Financial Planning for the Utterly Confused

Joel Lerner

Third Edition

McGraw-Hill, Inc.

New York St. Louis San Francisco Auckland Bogotá
Caracas Lisbon London Madrid Mexico Milan
Montreal New Delhi Paris San Juan São Paulo
Singapore Sydney Tokyo Toronto

*To the members of the middle
class—who pay for the tax shelters
of the rich as well as the social
programs of the poor*

Library of Congress Cataloging-in-Publication Data

Lerner, Joel J.
   Financial planning for the utterly confused / Joel Lerner.—3rd
ed.
      p.   cm.
   ISBN 0-07-037510-0 : —ISBN 0-07-037511-9(pbk.) :
   1. Finance, Personal—United States.   2. Investments—United
States.   I. Title.
HG179.L45 1991
332.024—dc20   91-3521
                                                         CIP

      6 7 8 9 0   DOC/DOC   9 7 6 5 4 3 2

ISBN 0-07-037510-0 {HC}
ISBN 0-07-037511-9 {PBK}

*The editors for this book were Theodore C. Nardin and Barbara Toniolo, the
editing supervisor was Olive H. Collen, and the production supervisor was
Pamela A. Pelton. It was set in Baskerville by Carol Woolverton, Lexington,
Mass.*

Printed and bound by R. R. Donnelley & Sons Company.

Contents

Preface   ix

Part 1. Financial Instruments from A to Z   1

1. Introduction to Financial Planning   3

How Do You Begin a Financial Plan?   3
How Does Age Enter into Financial Planning?   4
How Should You Deal with Financial Risk in Planning for
   the Future?   6
How Can You Overcome Obstacles to Your Financial Plan?   8
What Financial Records Should You Keep?   9
How Can Assets Be Owned?   10
How Does Financial Planning Differ for Women?   11
What Points Should You Remember?   14

2. Annuities for Today's Living   15

How Does an Annuity Work?   15
What Are the Different Characteristics of Annuities?   16
What Are the Risks Associated with Investing in Annuities?   19
What Are the Different Repayment Options Offered?   20
What Are the Tax Consequences of Annuities?   21

3. Certificates of Deposit—Old Faithful   22

How Does the Certificate of Deposit Work?   23
What Plans Should You Make When Purchasing a CD?   24
What Else Should You Know When Comparing CDs to
   Other Instruments?   26

4. Condominiums and Co-ops—
A Living Investment   29

What Is a Condominium?   30
What Are the Advantages and Disadvantages of
   Condominium Ownership?   31
What Is Needed in Order to Own a Condo?   32
What Is a Cooperative?   34
What Other Differences Should the Investor Know Of?   34

5. **Corporate Bond Market—For the Future**   37

How Do Corporate Bonds Work?   37
What Are the Characteristics of Bonds?   38
What Are the Different Types of Bonds?   39
What Factors Should You Consider When
  Purchasing Bonds?   41
How Do You Learn about Bonds?   44

6. **Ginnie Mae—The Misunderstood Instrument**   46

What Is a Ginnie Mae?   46
How Does the Ginnie Mae Work?   47
Are Ginnie Maes Safe?   48
How Is Income Paid to the Investor?   48
When Does the Ginnie Mae Mature?   50
How Do Current Interest Rates Affect the Ginnie Mae?   50
What Other Factors Should You Know About?   52
How Can the Small Investor Purchase a Ginnie Mae?   52

7. **Ginnie Mae Alternatives**   54

How Do Fannie Maes and Freddie Macs Work?   55
How Does the CMO Work?   55
How Do You Buy CMOs?   56
How Safe Are CMOs?   57

8. **Gold, Silver, and Diamonds—
   Investment or Enjoyment?**   58

Why Is Gold Considered an Investment?   58
Why Is Gold Considered Risky?   59
What Do the Numbers Mean?   60
What Are the Options for Investing in Gold?   60
What Is the Relation between Gold and Silver?   64
How Do You Purchase Silver for Investment Purposes?   64
How Do You Purchase Diamonds?   65
What Are the Major Drawbacks to Investing in Diamonds?   65
How Would You Summarize Investing in Precious Metals
  and Gems?   66

9. **Life Insurance—The Risk Protector**   67

What Is the Purpose of Life Insurance?   67

How Does Term Insurance Work? 68
How Does Straight Life Insurance Work? 69
How Does Universal Life Insurance Work? 70
How Does Single-Premium Whole Life Work? 71
What Should You Remember about Choosing a Policy? 73

10. Money Market Accounts—The Parking Lot 74

How Does a Money Market Account Work? 74
What Types of Money Market Funds Are Offered? 75
How Do Money Markets Issued by Banks Work? 77
What Are the Major Differences between the Money Market
Fund and the MMDA? 78
Are Both the Money Market Fund and the MMDA Safe
Investments? 79

11. Mortgages—The Finances of Home Ownership 81

What Must You Know about a Mortgage? 81
What Types of Mortgages Are Offered? 82
How Does the ARM Work? 82
How Does Refinancing a Mortgage Work in Today's
Market? 83
What Are the Tax Considerations in Mortgage Financing? 85
What Is a Home Equity Loan? 87

12. Municipal Bonds—The Tax-Free Choice 89

How Do Municipal Bonds Work? 89
What Types of Municipal Bonds Are Available? 90
What Are the Advantages and Disadvantages of
Municipal Bonds? 91
Are Municipals Your Best Investment? 92
Are Municipals a Risky Investment? 95
Can Municipal Bonds Be Called Back? 96
Are There Strategies in Purchasing Municipal Bonds? 96
How Do You Find the Best Bond Value? 97

**13. Municipal Trusts and Funds—Tax-Free
Alternatives 98**

What Are Municipal Funds and Trusts? 98
How Does the Unit Trust Work? 99
How Does the Municipal Fund Work? 100

How Does Insurance Affect the Trust or Fund?   101
What Are the Basic Differences between the Trust
  and the Fund?   101

14. Mutual Funds—Spreading the Risk   105

How Does the Mutual Fund Work?   105
What Are the Advantages of Mutual Fund Ownership?   106
What Are the Different Types of Mutual Funds?   109
What Are the Costs of Owning a Mutual Fund?   110
What Information Is Available?   113

15. Real Estate as Security and Investment   114

What Are the Benefits of Real Estate?   114
What Rules Govern Investing in Real Estate?   116
Is There an Alternative to a Direct Real Estate Purchase?   116
What Are the Tax Benefits of Selling a Home?   118

16. Stock Market—Bulls, Bears, and Pigs   120

How Does the Stock Market Work?   121
How Does an Investor Purchase Stock?   122
What Kinds of Stocks Are Available?   123
What Are the Advantages and Disadvantages of Stocks?   126

17. Stock Market Information—Where to Get It   128

How Do You Learn about Investing in the Stock Market?   128
What Statistics Should You Know to Evaluate Stocks?   130
What Is the Dow Jones Industrial Average?   133

18. Treasuries Are a Treasure   135

What Is the Best Method of Purchasing Treasury
  Obligations?   135
What Are Treasury Bills and How Do They Work?   138
Do You Receive a Certificate When You Purchase
  a T-Bill?   139
What Are Treasury Notes?   141
What Are Treasury Bonds?   142

19. U.S. Savings Bonds—Safety First   144

How Do EE Bonds Work?   145
How Do You Redeem Savings Bonds?   147

How Do Taxes Affect the Bonds? 149
What Role Do Bonds Play in Plans for College? 150
How Do HH Bonds Work? 152

20. Zero Investment 154

How Does the Zero Coupon Bond Work? 154
What Advantages Do Zeros Offer as an Investment? 156
Are Zero Coupon Bonds a Good Investment Vehicle
for Education? 157
What Are the Disadvantages of the Zero Coupon Bond? 158
What Is a Zero Coupon Municipal Bond? 159

Part 2. Financial Planning for the Future 161

21. Planning Your Retirement—An Overview 163

How Do Lump-Sum Distributions Work? 163
What Is the 5-Year Forward Average Plan? 164
What Is an IRA Rollover? 164
Which Method—5-Year Averaging or IRA Rollover—
Is Better? 165
How Does Early Retirement Play a Role in the
Various Plans? 165

22. The IRA 168

How Does the IRA Work? 168
What Are the Tax Consequences of the IRA? 170
What Are the Rules for IRA Distributions? 171
What Happens If You Die before You Use Your
IRA Funds? 173
What Investment Options Are Available for an IRA? 174
How Should You Choose among These Investment
Options? 175
Is the IRA Transferable to Other Investments? 176

23. The 401(k) Plan 177

How Does the 401(k) Differ from an Ordinary IRA? 177
How Does the 401(k) Work? 178
What about Withdrawal from a 401(k)? 179

24. The Simplified Employee Pension (SEP)   180

How Does the SEP Work?   180
What Should You Know about the SEP?   181
Has the Tax Reform Act Changed the SEP?   182

25. The Keogh Plan   183

How Does the Keogh Plan Work?   183
What Are the Differences between the Keogh
and the IRA?   184
How Do You Qualify for a Keogh Plan?   184

26. Social Security   186

How Do Social Security Payments Work under the
Tax Law?   186
What Can You Do to Offset This Law?   188
What Happens if You Want to Retire before Age 65?   189
How Do You Know You Are Getting Accurate Social
Security Benefits?   190
Are There Any Penalties if You Work Part-time after
You Retire?   190
What Are the Family Benefits of a Social Security Plan?   191
How Does Divorce Affect Spousal Benefits?   192
How Does the Death of the Insured Affect Social Security
Payments?   192
How Are Children Affected by Social Security?   193

27. Will It?   194

What Is a Will?   194
Who Carries Out the Instructions in a Will?   195
How Do You Begin to Draw Up a Will?   196
How Can You Be Certain That the Distribution of the
Estate Will Be without Problems?   197
What Happens if You Die without a Will?   199
Are There Any Alternatives to Having a Will?   200

Epilogue   203
Glossary   204

Preface

I am a teacher, not a stockbroker, bank executive, or insurance salesperson. My specialty isn't fancy jargon, hucksterism, or statistics. Rather, it's explaining financial and economic matters to ordinary people in plain English. That's what *Financial Planning for the Utterly Confused* is all about.

The larger portion of this book (Part 1) consists of an easy-to-read, alphabetically arranged listing of the various kinds of investments—financial instruments, as they are called—which the typical investor is likely to be interested in. You won't find tips on high-flying stocks that promise to help you double your money overnight. As you already know, no one can make such promises with any certainty. What you will find here is an honest appraisal of the advantages, disadvantages, costs, and benefits of each type of financial instrument—an appraisal based on current tax laws and their effects upon you, the investor.

Part 1 will inform you of the various financial instruments that are available today, breaking each down into understandable reading.

Part 2 discusses financial planning for that inevitable time of retirement, covering topics that every individual must understand in order to make the latter years ones of joy rather than struggle.

A glossary of common financial terms is provided to serve as a handy reference tool as you read the money-managing columns in your daily newspaper or your favorite magazine. It should help you penetrate some of the verbal fog generated by brokers, bankers, and salespeople.

My hope is that *Financial Planning for the Utterly Confused* will be a valuable tool for the millions of Americans who need help in managing their small- to medium-sized investment plans. The information in this book can be the first building block in the creation of a secure and comfortable financial future that only you can initiate. There is a saying that sums up financial planning in 10 two-letter words:

> If it is to be
> It is up to me.

Joel Lerner

About the Author

Joel Lerner is a professor and former chairman of the Business Division at Sullivan County Community College, Loch Sheldrake, New York. He is the publisher of the *Middle/Fixed Income Letter,* a monthly personal financial newsletter, and has authored numerous textbooks that have sold more than a half million copies. Mr. Lerner is a financial lecturer to several *Fortune* 500 firms, has produced his own TV and radio series, and addresses thousands of people every year on financial management. He lives in Monticello, New York.

PART 1

Financial Instruments from A to Z

1

Introduction to Financial Planning

Money never changes, only pockets.

The best investment you can make is in yourself. Financially you must have some knowledge about your own affairs because you cannot hand over everything to some financial adviser or broker and expect that person to do it all. Each month you no doubt receive a monthly statement of your financial position, but do you really have any idea what those transactions mean? If you will take the time to learn about money matters, you will receive a rich reward—dividends in understanding that in the long run will improve your financial position.

How Do You Begin a Financial Plan?

To begin a financially secured plan, your personal and family financial goals must be identified. Goals are based on what is most important to you. Short-term goals (up to a year) are things you desire soon (household appliances), while long-term goals are items you want later on in life (a home, education for your children, sufficient retirement income). Take these short- and long-term goals and put them into an order of priority, making sure you have an emergency fund as the first item. Then estimate the cost of each goal and set a target

3

date to reach the goal. Don't forget to consider the high cost of inflation (see Table 1.1) because it most certainly will affect your long-term goals.

You are all aware of the changing life cycle. Your goals must be updated as your needs and circumstances change. In your early years, short-term goals may include adequate insurance, establishing good credit, and just getting under way. During your middle years, the goals shift from immediate personal spending to education for children and planning for retirement. In latter years, travel may become a primary goal. Although every financial plan will be different, each should meet certain criteria:

1. An emergency fund equal to 3 months of net income (after taxes).

2. Specific amounts for investments set aside on a regular basis.

3. Adequate insurance.

Also, when planning for your future, consider age as a vital factor.

How Does Age Enter into Financial Planning?

Here are some guidelines to use depending on your present age:

Age 20 to 40: When you are young, growth should be your primary goal; a relatively high degree of risk is tolerable. Suggestion: Invest in a diversified portfolio of common stocks or in a mutual fund managed for growth of assets, not income. Speculation (real estate, coins, metals, etc.) is acceptable.

Age 40 to 50: Stocks are still an attractive choice, but now you need a more balanced approach. Begin to invest in fixed-rate instruments (bonds) and look into ones that are tax-free (municipals).

Age 50 to 60: At this point, growth is less important, risk less acceptable. Move your investments out of stocks and into bonds, in order to minimize risk and increase your current flow of income.

Age 60 and over: By now, all funds should be in income-producing investments with maturities of 5 years and less. This will provide safety and maximum current interest.

When you plan investments for your age bracket, consider the following:

1. *Security of principal:* This refers to the preservation of your original capital. Treasury bills are guaranteed by the government while stocks fluctuate greatly.

2. *Return:* This means the money you earn on your investment (interest, dividends, profit).

3. *Liquidity:* This deals with the ease of converting your investment into cash.

4. *Convenience:* This refers to the time and energy you are willing to expend on your investment.

5. *Tax status:* Depending on your tax bracket, each investment will bear heavily on your personal situation. Municipal bonds are tax-free while CDs are fully taxable.

6. *Your personal circumstances:* Included under this category would be your age, your income, your health, your individual circumstances, and your ability to tolerate risk.

How Should You Deal with Financial Risk in Planning for the Future?

As you'll learn, the single most important factor in deciding on the best investments for you is the level of risk you can afford to take. Thus, the first step in formulating your investment plan is a careful self-examination. How much money do you have to invest? How great will your financial needs be for the foreseeable future? How much of your capital can you realistically afford to risk losing? And how great a degree of risk can you and your family handle psychologically? Each of these factors will have bearing on the degree of risk you can tolerate in your investment decisions. The sudden invasion of Kuwait and the Persian Gulf War, which followed, brought about numerous changes in investment philosophies and risk and safety concepts.

The trade-off is simple: to get larger rewards you have to take greater risks. Every investor must find a comfort-zone balance of security and risk. You can achieve a balance by investing in a pyramid fashion: Begin with conservative (safe) investments at the foundation (Treasury obligations, insured money markets, CDs) and then gradually build up, accepting a bit more risk at each step. At the very top, you may have high-risk investments (coins, gold, real estate), but because of the pyramid, the investment will be small compared to the rest of your holdings. Also, to minimize loss, you should have at least two different types of investments that perform differently during a specific period of time. For example, when interest rates are low, stocks usually gain while money markets do poorly. Diversify! A series of guidelines for handling risk follows:

1. Don't invest in any instrument in which you can lose more than you can potentially gain. This factor is sometimes referred to as *risk-reward balance.*

2. Diversify your holdings. Spread your investment dollars among a variety of instruments, thereby minimizing the risk potential.

3. When investments fail to perform up to your expectations (the period to hold them is based upon your objectives), sell them. "Cutting your losses" is the only sure way to prevent minor setbacks from turning into financial nightmares. A rule of thumb is to sell when the value declines by 10 percent of your original cost.

4. Don't discount risk altogether. The rewards may justify "taking a chance." Remember that it is a wise person who lives with money in the bank. It's a fool who dies that way.

How Can You Overcome Obstacles to Your Financial Plan?

Regardless of how well you financially plan, certain obstacles will always arise. Four factors that could have a major impact on your investment objectives are as follows:

1. *Inflation:* It is obvious that if you are to plan financially for your future, you must receive a return that is high enough to outpace any long-term effects of inflation. If, for example, you kept retirement money in a savings account paying 5½ percent per year and over the same period of time the inflation rate averaged 6 percent per year, your investment would have less purchasing power at retirement than it did when it was started. Table 1.1 is designed to illustrate the effect of the inflation rate on the cost of living for future years. Look down the column to the number of years until you retire and read across to the column under the estimated inflation rate. Multiply your plan or budget by that number to adjust for future costs. For example, if you are planning to retire in 10 years and the inflation rate is 5 percent, multiply your cost of investment or budget by 1.629 in order to reflect inflated adjusted costs. Ten years from now it would cost you $65,160 to buy the same items you could have bought today for $40,000 ($40,000 × 1.629 = $65,160).

2. *Interest rate risk:* A change in interest rates will cause the price of fixed-rate instruments (bonds) to move in the opposite direction of interest rates. If interest rates go down, the value of bonds goes up, and, conversely, if interest rates go up, the value of the bonds goes down. You have interest rate risk with all types of bonds. The longer the maturity of the bond, the greater the interest rate risk, so if you are concerned about this risk, stay short-term.

TABLE 1.1. EFFECT OF INFLATION RATE ON COST OF LIVING IN FUTURE YEARS

Years to retire- ment	Inflation Rate							
	3%	4%	5%	6%	7%	8%	9%	10%
1	1.030	1.040	1.050	1.060	1.070	1.080	1.090	1.100
2	1.061	1.082	1.103	1.124	1.145	1.166	1.188	1.210
3	1.093	1.125	1.158	1.191	1.225	1.260	1.285	1.331
4	1.126	1.170	1.216	1.262	1.311	1.360	1.412	1.464
5	1.159	1.217	1.276	1.338	1.403	1.469	1.539	1.611
6	1.194	1.265	1.340	1.419	1.501	1.587	1.677	1.772
7	1.230	1.316	1.407	1.504	1.606	1.714	1.828	1.949
8	1.267	1.369	1.477	1.594	1.718	1.851	1.993	2.144
9	1.305	1.423	1.551	1.689	1.838	1.999	2.172	2.358
10	1.344	1.480	1.629	1.791	1.967	2.159	2.367	2.594
11	1.384	1.539	1.710	1.898	2.105	2.332	2.580	2.853
12	1.426	1.601	1.796	2.012	2.252	2.518	2.813	3.138
13	1.469	1.665	1.886	2.133	2.410	2.720	3.066	3.452
14	1.513	1.732	1.980	2.261	2.579	3.937	3.342	3.797
15	1.558	1.801	2.079	2.397	2.759	3.172	3.642	4.177
16	1.605	1.873	2.183	2.540	2.952	3.426	3.970	4.595
17	1.653	1.948	2.292	2.693	3.159	3.700	4.328	5.054
18	1.702	2.026	2.407	2.854	3.380	3.996	4.717	5.560
19	1.754	2.107	2.527	3.026	3.617	4.316	5.142	6.116
20	1.806	2.191	2.653	3.207	3.870	4.661	5.604	6.727
25	2.094	2.666	3.386	4.292	5.427	6.848	8.623	10.835
30	2.427	3.243	4.322	5.743	7.612	10.063	13.268	17.449

3. *Taxation:* Determining to what extent any tax-advantaged investment would help you is a serious consideration. You must therefore take into account your tax bracket, present income, future income, and investment holdings before you do financial planning.

4. *Procrastination:* This is an obstacle that depends solely on you. Don't imitate the person who says, "Someday I'm going to stop procrastinating." Regardless of how well a financial plan is structured, if you don't follow it through, it will be doomed before it begins. Therefore, discipline yourself by continuing regular investing. Remember, it wasn't raining when Noah built his ark. Don't wait.

Now that your goals have been defined and the areas of risks and rewards examined, the next step is getting all the "paper" together.

What Financial Records Should You Keep?

Start by developing a "road map" so that you or your heirs (in case of disability or death) will know where documents are. Records that should be kept available are:

1. Professional numbers: Telephone numbers of your lawyer, doctor, accountant, insurance company, business associates, and financial adviser or broker.

2. Account numbers: Brokerage, bank, credit cards, insurance policies (and beneficiaries), and safe deposit box (keys and authorized deputies).

3. All business records (tax returns, company books, payroll data, etc.).

4. An updated will and trust agreements, if any.

5. Retirement benefits: Social security, Keogh plans, Simplified employee pension plans (SEPs), 401(k)s, etc.

6. Burial arrangements: cemetery plot, deeds.

7. Any outstanding liabilities.

The next area of financial planning is an understanding of the various forms of ownership.

How Can Assets Be Owned?

In order for you to financially plan, you must understand the concept of ownership. Joint ownership is the most common method by which married couples take title to their house and other assets. It may also be used by others who wish to share the control of some property. Let's examine the three basic types of joint ownership, each of which has certain special legal and financial characteristics you should know about.

1. *Joint tenancy:* With this type of ownership, both owners have a complete and undivided interest in the property. Neither owner can sell or transfer his or her interest in the property without the consent of the other owner. When one owner dies, the property immediately passes to the surviving owner without having to go to probate (the acceptance of the will of the deceased by an appropriate court). For joint tenancy to be in effect, the names of both owners must appear on the deed or other ownership document.

Both married couples and single people use joint tenancy as a method of guaranteeing ease of transfer of property upon the death of one of the owners. However, it can't be considered a substitute for a will. As an illustration, joint tenancy may not automatically produce the desired result after death. For example, suppose you and your sister buy a summer home together, taking title as joint tenants. You die first, and your sister dies shortly thereafter. Upon your death, your share in the summer home reverts immediately to your sister. Therefore, when she dies, the home goes entirely to her heirs; your own heirs will receive no share in it. This may or may not be what you intended.

2. *Tenancy in common:* With this type of ownership, each owner has title to half the property. If one owner dies, his or her share does not automatically pass to the survivor. Instead, it is disposed of in accordance with the will of the deceased. This method is used by friends or relatives who wish to form a joint ownership and share in its benefits while they are alive but want to retain the right to decide individually what happens to their share of the property when they die.

3. *Community property:* In certain states, husband and wife share equally in any property either one accumulates while they are living together. This is so regardless of whose name appears on the deed or ownership papers. Such jointly owned property is called *community property,* and the states where this is a matter of law are called *community property states* (Arizona, California, Idaho, Louisiana, Nevada, New Mexico, Texas, Washington, and Wisconsin). There are exceptions under the law to community property: (1) property obtained by either spouse prior to the marriage; (2) property acquired after marriage by gift or inheritance; and (3) property acquired in non-community property states. Note that the fact that you have moved from a community property state to a non-community property state does not automatically exempt you and your spouse from the community property law. You are still subject to the law for property you obtained while married and a resident of the community property state.

How Does Financial Planning Differ for Women?

Here's a statistic that may surprise you: Out of all females over the age of 21, approximately 85 percent will die as single women. How is this possible? Out of every 100 women, 6 never marry; of the remaining 94, 33 have marriages that end in divorce and 46 outlive their husbands. The implication is simple: The chances are excellent that at some time in a woman's life, she will be alone and forced to manage her own finances. If you're presently single, you already understand this. If you're married, please read on.

If you are a married woman, it is essential that you consider yourself financially separate from your husband. This is so even though he may supply most of your family's income and handle many or most of the financial decisions. You should make a financial plan of your own and provide for the likelihood that eventually you'll be managing your money independently.

A good place to start is by opening personal checking and savings accounts and obtaining one or more credit cards in your name only. Why is this necessary? Because a woman whose assets are entirely tied up in joint accounts with her husband, and whose credit cards are all in her husband's name, may face severe financial problems in the future. If you become divorced or widowed, your credit history will be based entirely on your husband's finances, not your own. You may learn, to your dismay, that you lack the financial standing to qualify for your own line of credit. When financial need strikes, this can be a devastating handicap.

Furthermore, any money held in a joint account with your husband may be frozen by the bank or financial institution upon his death, leaving you with no access to funds until after your husband's estate is settled. And in the event of divorce, you may find that all jointly held funds are divided equally, even though you may have contributed more to some accounts.

The point, then, is that married women, whether working outside the home or not, must plan for retirement independently of their husbands. You should develop your own savings and investment plan with a definite goal to be attained by retirement age. You should open your own individual retirement account, invested in financial instruments appropriate for your age and income. And you should become as fully informed about your family's finances as your husband.

Every woman should have her own will and keep it up to date. It could even be argued that a wife's will is more essential than her husband's since, in most cases, she will outlive him and thus be responsible for not one but two estates—his and hers. This is so even when a wife has few assets of her own. Consider this scenario: A husband dies, leaving all his property to his wife. Shortly afterward, she dies *intestate,* that is, without a will. All the family's assets would be disposed of according to the laws of intestacy applicable in her state. The results may or may not be in accordance with her wishes.

Also, consider what happens in the event of the death of or separation from the husband. What can you do financially to protect what you own should you decide to remarry? Here are some possibilities.

1. A prenuptial agreement can help you by allowing you to keep any assets out of the hands of your new spouse if something should happen to the new marriage (death, divorce, etc.). Newly married couples may feel that this written agreement shows a lack of trust, but in truth it actually helps keep family harmony. I have seen adult children's concerns (the new husband may get all their mother's money) put aside by the use of the prenuptial agreement. To play it safe, hire different lawyers to represent each party in drafting this agreement.

2. Consider the consequences of remarrying and its effect on social security benefits. If you are a widow under age 60 and are collecting social security benefits based upon your late husband's social security account, remarriage will stop your benefits. However, if you wait until age 60 or later, you will then be able to draw on your new mate's social security account or your late spouse's account, whichever is greater.

3. If you are over age 55, you are entitled to a one-time capital-gains exclusion (up to $125,000) on the sale of your home (see the last section of Chapter 15). Married couples can take this advantage only once even if each owns a home. Therefore, before remarrying, you should consider selling your home and your intended's home so that

you will get two exclusions (a total of $250,000) instead of one.

What Points Should You Remember?

This introduction to financial planning lays the foundation for all the topics in the forthcoming pages of this book. You owe it to yourself to learn as much about personal finances as possible, so that when the time comes for financial decisions to be made, you'll be prepared. And that applies to everyone—male, female, age 21 or 71. You must understand how the many different financial instruments operate and how they will directly affect your financial future. Read (newspapers, magazines, annual reports), learn (seminars, courses), ask (brokers, financial planners), and make certain that you can apply the knowledge gained from reading the following chapters so that when opportunity does knock, you are not in the backyard looking for four-leaf clovers.

2

Annuities for Today's Living

Forever is a long time, but not as long as it was yesterday.

Time certainly flies. It was only a few years ago that the government introduced the Tax Reform Act (TRA), which has had a profound effect on many people's investment philosophy and tax planning. For example, with the loss of the IRA deduction to many taxpayers, there is little that the middle-income investor can use as a tax deferment and tax deduction. The insurance industry's offering of the annuity has become a serious alternative for investors who wish to look for deferred income, possible tax deduction, and safety of investment.

How Does an Annuity Work?

When you retire, you will want to be able to live comfortably for life on the income from your investments. However, because of modern medicine, many people run the risk of outliving their investment income. As a possible solution to this problem, consider purchasing an annuity.

An annuity may be considered the opposite of a traditional insurance policy. When you buy insurance, you agree to pay annual premiums to an insurance company. In return, the company will pay the face value of the policy in a lump sum to your beneficiaries when you die. By contrast, when you buy an annuity, you pay the company a sum of money and, in return, receive a monthly income for as long as you live. Naturally, the longer you live, the more money you'll receive. You might say that life insurance protects you against financial loss as a result of dying too soon, while an annuity protects you against financial loss as a result of living too long.

What Are the Different Characteristics of Annuities?

There are several different types of annuities. They can be categorized according to three main characteristics:

1. *Premiums.* The cost of the annuity will depend on many factors:

- How much you will contribute to your account
- The rate of return earned by the fund
- The length of time the money is left in the fund
- The procedure for distribution of the funds to beneficiaries (note that options can raise or lower your monthly annuity return)

An annuity may be purchased either through a single lump-sum premium or through annual premium payments. If you happen to have a large sum of money to invest at one time—for example, from an inheritance or from a pension fund—you may want to purchase an annuity with a lump-sum payment. This is known as a *single premium deferred annuity* (SPDA). Once you have made the initial investment, no further contribution is required. An SPDA is a basic annuity that works in the following way: You buy a contract and pay a lump sum ($2500 to $500,000) that guarantees future payments. If you die before you begin to receive withdrawals, the policy will pay the estate the contract's face value plus interest. If you live past age 59½, you may begin your withdrawal program or you may cash in the policy and receive your principal plus all interest earned on it tax-deferred. This is similar to a nondeductible IRA since the income earned stays tax-deferred in the annuity until it is withdrawn; yet it is better than an IRA because you are not limited to a $2000 maximum yearly deposit.

Annuity income payments depend on life expectancy and are thus classified as life insurance. This is important for you to understand because the classification allows the annuity's investment earnings to be treated as tax-deferred, with no tax on the annuity's accumulation until the money is withdrawn. This is surprising since well over 95 percent of the annuity is investment while only a very small balance is for insurance. But watch out if you withdraw before age 59½. Except in the case of death or disability, a premature withdrawal will cost you an IRS penalty of 10 percent (known as *excise tax*). There is also an insurance company surrender penalty (in some cases) of 7 percent of your investment if you withdraw it during the first year; 6 percent during the second year; 5 percent during the third year; and so on. From the eighth year on, no penalty is charged. Make sure you find out about surrender charges before deciding on where to invest in an annuity, and be sure to ask your agent or broker about sales charges (if there are any) before you buy. These charges could affect your total yield and future income. Most companies charge annual administrative fees which further reduce your income. These fees vary, but they average around 1.5 percent of the amount invested. Find out the amount of the fee before you invest, and compare the rates charged by several companies. These fees are important in determining the annuity to be chosen because they directly affect its yield. The Securities and Exchange Commission (SEC) has issued new rules that now require the annuity companies to show their charges in a standardized table located near the beginning of the information booklet (prospectus). These charges could include:

Front-end sales commissions
Annual maintenance costs
Annual mortality and expense charges

Annual investment advisory fees
Surrender charges

2. *Payment return.* An annuity may provide for either immediate return to the investor or deferred return. An immediate annuity is purchased at the time you want to start receiving income, and it requires a single lump-sum premium. The insurance company begins sending you monthly checks right away. One caution: When you buy an immediate annuity, you forfeit all liquidity; that is, you can't change your mind and withdraw your money from the investment. A deferred annuity, on the other hand, is purchased prior to the time when income is needed (deferred period). During this period, which may be very short or may last as long as 40 years, your investment earns interest tax-free. If you should decide to cancel your annuity before withdrawal time, you may have to pay a surrender charge, which will vary from company to company.

3. *Return on investment.* Annuities may be classified as either *fixed-dollar* or *variable.* Fixed-dollar annuities guarantee you a certain minimum interest rate. The actual rate you'll receive is fixed for only a few months or years, but there is a minimum rate below which your return cannot drop. Insurance companies usually invest fixed-dollar annuity funds in highly secured investments such as government bonds. With a fixed-dollar annuity, you'll know that your principal is secure and that you'll receive at least a specified minimum income. Some companies will offer what is known as a "bailout" provision in their annuity contract which states that if the annuity fails to earn a specified interest rate, the holder can withdraw his or her money without penalty. Also, if that were the case and you could find a competing annuity with a high yield, you would be allowed to transfer the funds with no tax penalty. This procedure is known as a *1035 exchange* and would be treated in the same manner as the rollover of an IRA. Variable annuities, on the other hand, are usually invested in more risky, but potentially more lucrative, instruments. The amount of interest your money earns, and therefore the size of the payments you'll receive, will vary

according to the success of the insurance company's investments. In addition, your principal is not untouchable. For example, a market disaster could wipe out part of your investment. There was a major negative impact on the values of
annuities immediately after the October 1987 and 1989 stock
market crashes, even immediately after the invasion of Kuwait
and its aftermath in 1990 and 1991. Therefore, although you
may earn more with a variable annuity, the risk you take is
greater.

What Are the Risks Associated with Investing in Annuities?

Stated simply, avoid annuities with extremely high rates of return, as those rates could be generated from investments in
junk bonds. Although the junk bond market did very well in
the late 1980s, because of the many mergers and acquisitions,
the early 1990s saw a reversal. Many savings and loan failures
during this period were attributed to junk bonds. As a rule of
thumb, stay away from an annuity company that invests more
than 20 percent of its bond portfolio in issues that are rated
BB or lower. Whichever type of annuity you choose, your ability to tolerate risk should be the deciding factor. Younger people may move toward the variable annuity because they may
feel that there will be enough time to recoup any possible
losses, whereas older people may choose fixed-rate annuities
because of the guaranteed yield. Regardless of which type you
choose, insurance products are still among the safest savings
plans around because of the strict state regulations of insurance investments. Look at companies that consistently earn
an A (excellent) or A+ (superior) rating from A. M. Best Co.
or AAA by Standard & Poor's, and, if possible, read through
the literature concerning the company's investment holdings. Certain companies offering high yields may be investing
their funds in junk bonds and other high-risk areas and thus
may not be able to maintain those yields or even competitive
rates over the long term. If ratings and yields are important

to you, you can request (from the salesperson) a copy of the most recent quarterly survey done by Variable Annuity Research & Data Service (VARDS). This Miami company gives an accurate performance rating (after subtracting the effect of all fees, except annual maintenance) of each annuity.

What Are the Different Repayment Options Offered?

As noted, with an annuity, the longer you live, the greater the return you can expect to earn. This means, of course, that if you die early, you may never earn the amount you originally paid for the annuity. Because of the different needs of investors, there are several repayment options from which to choose:

1. *Individual life annuity.* Here, payments (which are the highest of any option) are continued throughout your life with no further payments made after you die even if you should die only a year or two after payments begin. This plan is designed only for a person who wants the highest amount of regular income and has no spouse or other dependents who might need financial support after the annuitant dies.

2. *Joint-survivor annuity.* This plan provides monthly payments for as long as either you or your spouse lives. In other words, at your demise, your spouse would continue receiving payments until he or she died. It is obvious that the payouts each month will be smaller than the individual life annuity because the payments extend to two lives and therefore will have to stretch over a longer period.

3. *Guaranteed-minimum annuity.* Under the terms of this annuity, there is a minimum payout period established. In the event that the annuity holder dies shortly after the payouts begin, more payments will be made to the beneficiaries for a specified period of time. For example, an investor

might buy this type of policy in order to receive payments for the rest of his or her life but wants to make certain that the insurance company will make payments for, say, at least 10 years. This is known as a "10-year certain contract." If the investor dies after receiving 2 years of payouts, he or she will be assured that whoever is designated as the beneficiary will receive money for the next 8 years. For this privilege, the investor will receive a smaller payback (about 6 percent less than from the other previously mentioned options).

What Are the Tax Consequences of Annuities?

Annuities provide certain income tax benefits that are of special benefit to middle-class investors. You'll find that your assets accumulate more quickly than with most other investments because the interest you earn is not subject to income tax until you begin to withdraw it. In other words, you can save in three ways:

1. Your principal earns interest.
2. That interest earns interest.
3. You earn interest on the money you save in current taxes.

Annuities have certain other distinct advantages. The most important benefit lies in the fact that annuity income is guaranteed for life, no matter how long you live. It's pretty comforting to retire with an income that you know will always be there. Also, when death does occur, regardless of the payout plan you choose, the annuity is free from probate because an annuity is an insurance product having a named beneficiary with the proceeds going directly to the designated heirs, bypassing court costs, legal fees, and long delays. And on the topic of life and death, never worry about life being short because life is too short for that.

3

Certificates of Deposit— Old Faithful

It may not seem as exciting as trading in pork bellies, but it always brings home the bacon.

At one time, you needed $100,000 or more to invest in a bank *certificate of deposit.* This restriction had been established by the Federal Reserve Board in order to protect savings banks, savings and loan institutions, and credit unions from competition with commercial banks. The fear was that if commercial banks could issue high-yielding certificates of deposit in small denominations, small savers would withdraw their funds from low-yielding passbook savings accounts in order to buy the certificates. This, in turn, would adversely affect the savings banks, most of whose holdings were tied up in low-yielding, long-term mortgages. In effect, the Federal Reserve sought to protect the banks at the expense of small savers.

All this changed after 1973, when the first money market mutual fund offered its shares for sale for as little as $1000. Money market funds, which paid rates comparable to those offered on bank certificates, quickly became a favorite investment for small savers. The savings banks began to lose customers. As a result, the banks themselves demanded that the rules be changed so as to allow them to compete with the money market funds. Thus was born the certificate of deposit (CD) for the small investor.

Today, most federal restrictions governing insured time deposits in banks have been lifted as banks are free to compete with one another in setting terms for their own CDs. You can now buy a CD from a savings and loan institution, a savings bank, a credit union, a commercial bank, or a broker (though under a proposed Treasury bank plan, stockbrokers would be prohibited from selling them). The competition among these suppliers tends to keep rates high, and for the small saver, the revolution of the 1970s and 1980s has certainly been beneficial, though through 1990, rates eased off considerably.

How Does the Certificate of Deposit Work?

The concept of the CD is simple. It is a savings instrument issued by a financial institution which pays you interest at a guaranteed rate for a specified term. When the CD reaches maturity, you will receive your principal and all interest earned. Unlike bond interest (paid periodically) the interest from a CD usually compounds, which means you will be earning interest on your interest. The amount you invest in a CD is insured by the federal government for up to $100,000 (because of this insurance ceiling, proposals are being introduced to limit all bank accounts to $100,000). However, it is not wise to put the entire $100,000 in one account since the federal insurance ceiling applies to both principal and interest. I suggest that you have no more than $85,000 to $90,000 in any single certificate because any interest you earn on the CD could increase your balance, surpassing the maximum insured sum and thereby not being automatically protected if the bank should fail. Just keep this in mind when thinking of federally insured funds:

Your money is safe, so do not fret
Backed by the government trillions in debt

What Plans Should You Make When Purchasing a CD?

There are two primary considerations in planning your investment in a CD: (1) the term of the investment and (2) the rate of return.

1. *Term:* The most popular type of CD is the 6-month certificate, but CDs are available with maturities ranging from 7 days to 10 years. During the term of your CD, the money you've invested is relatively costly to liquidate (illiquid). If an emergency arises which requires you to withdraw your money before maturity (reservists and their families found this to be the case in 1990 and 1991), you'll be penalized for it. This penalty is known as *EWP* (*early withdrawal penalty*) and will vary from bank to bank. Thus, you'll want to consider carefully when you're likely to need the money before you invest in a CD. If a college tuition bill is due to be paid in 1 year and 3 months, you know that you'll want a certificate which matures at that time. It may pay for you to buy CDs in smaller denominations instead of purchasing one large certificate. Remember, you never know what the future holds, and at some time you may need to withdraw a portion of the funds. For example, if you were to buy a $50,000 one-year CD and 8 months later you needed about $10,000, some banks would charge you a penalty on the entire $50,000 since you would have to cash in the full CD. You would have been wiser to have purchased five $10,000 CDs, thus having to break only one of them, leaving the other four intact. And the interest rate is usually the same on five smaller certificates ($10,000 each) as it is on one larger one ($50,000).

2. *Rate of return:* The interest paid on a CD will vary not only according to the term of the certificate but also from time to time (as interest rates fluctuate) as well as from bank to bank. Don't buy your CD at the first bank you visit; the competing bank across the street may well be offering half a point more. Shop around! Ask about how the bank cred-

its the interest earned to your account. The more frequently interest is credited, the better for you, since each time your account grows through an interest payment, the amount of money you have working for you grows as well. Over the term of a CD, the differences among accounts can be substantial. Here's an example: A $10,000 deposit at a rate of 8.5 percent interest will earn $850 if there is no compounding. If interest is credited to the account quarterly, the amount earned increases to $877. With monthly compounding, the interest earned is $883, and with daily compounding, $900. So do investigate these policies. If you find a bank that compounds your interest daily, you may want to do your investing there. In their advertising, banks will sometimes reflect their compounding policies by listing a true rate of return (known as the *effective annual yield*) along with the no-compounding nominal rate (known as the *interest rate*) for a given CD. Thus a CD with an interest rate of 8.05 percent may pay an effective annual yield of 8.32 percent. Use the effective rate, if available, for comparison purposes.

Also, for comparison purposes, look at this scenario. An investment company proudly states that its instrument has had an average annual return of 20 percent a year for the last 10 years. Sounds great? Not necessarily. The investment increased 200 percent (20% × 10 years) over the decade, based upon simple interest. But this 20 percent earns only 11.6 percent compounded interest.

If you want to compare the simple and compound rate return and don't have a compound interest table, try this formula:

$$A = P(1 + r)^t$$

where A = amount of money you'll have at the end of a specific period of time

P = principal

r = rate of interest

t = time period

For example, a $1000 investment that yields 10 percent in 4 years compounded annually would produce $1464:

$$A = 1000(1 + 0.10)^4$$

$$A = 1000(1.10)^4 \quad \text{or} \quad 1000(1.10 \times 1.10 \times 1.10 \times 1.10)$$

$$A = 1464$$

What Else Should You Know When Comparing CDs to Other Instruments?

Here are some other points to consider when shopping for the best deal on a CD:

- Ask about variable-rate CDs. These rates are usually based on the current rates on Treasury bills issued by the federal government. They may be higher or lower than the rates paid on fixed-rate CDs, depending on financial conditions. These variable rates are designed for people who believe that interest rates will rise. If the ups and downs of these variable rates concern you, stagger your maturity dates. In this way, as you receive your principal back, you will be able to reinvest it in higher-yielding CDs, if rates have gone up, or in another investment, if rates have fallen.

- Ask whether you can increase the size of your investment after the original purchase of your CD has been made. This can be advantageous if you expect more funds to be available shortly (and if you expect interest rates to decline in the future).

- Don't forget that since 1982 brokers have also been able to offer CDs. The certificates sold by brokers are units, usually in denominations of $1000 or more, of larger certificates issued by savings institutions. Broker-sold CDs have one major advantage over those purchased directly from banks. Brokers are not required to charge a penalty on early withdrawal of invested funds. If you wish, you can sell your CD back to the broker at the current market rate without incurring any penalty. This form of liquidity could be very important, as it affords you the opportunity to participate in an upward move of interest rates. However, there may be a fee imposed for selling your CDs before maturity, so weigh the options carefully. Also, brokered CDs may not carry compound interest (which would lower their effective yield), so ask questions of your broker before committing any funds. As of this writing, broker-generated CDs were being debated in Congress, and it is possible that brokers will not continue offering them.

- Inquire about some new types of bank CDs. For example:

1. *Odd terms:* This type offers unusual lengths of time until maturity (7 months, 13 months, etc.), which, by the way, makes it very difficult to compare yields to other instruments.
2. *No early withdrawal penalty:* Although not usually known to the general public, new federal regulations no longer require banks to charge a penalty on premature withdrawals. Although most banks still charge an EWP, some are now offering a no-penalty CD. However, these "no penalties" may pay a lower interest rate than the traditional CDs; so compare both yields to determine whether the no-penalty clause is worth the difference.
3. *Step-ups:* This type of CD pays a rising rate of interest periodically (usually every 6 months) if interest rates rise. *Warning:* Watch out when you see advertisements about these "step-ups," because the banks usually quote only the last (which is the highest) rate, which does not represent all the earlier interest rates you received while holding onto these CDs.
4. *Bump-ups:* This is a variation on a step-up that permits the owner of the CD to ask for a rate increase once during the life of the certificate.

- Know what questions to ask of your banker or broker before buying:

1. I am not concerned about yield or rate, but how much money will I receive at maturity?
2. What, if any, is the early withdrawal penalty and how is it applied?
3. Do I get a better rate if I am a current bank customer?
4. Are there higher rates offered for larger deposits that will still be covered by federal insurance?

In addition, when considering buying CDs, compare them to such similar investment instruments as Treasury notes. On the one hand, a Treasury note pays interest which is free of state and local taxes, unlike the CD whose earnings are fully taxable. On the other hand, the market value of a long-term Treasury note can decline drastically if interest rates rise. With a CD, a sharp increase in interest rates can be much less painful. The worst that can happen is a partial loss of interest, in the event you decide to withdraw your investment before maturity in order to take advantage of the new higher rates available. The more lucrative investment into which you shift your funds will probably more than make up for that loss. So look carefully at your alternatives before making a decision.

Given all these factors, it seems safe to say that the bank CD—with its high degree of safety, competitive rate of return, and flexibility as to maturity—will remain a deservedly popular investment choice for the foreseeable future. And on the topic of money, it's true that you can't take it with you, but where can you go without it?

4

Condominiums and Co-ops—A Living Investment

Rents are so high now, leases are breaking tenants.

If you live in a rented apartment, you probably realize that owning your own home would provide you with some important financial advantages. For one thing, there are substantial tax benefits associated with mortgage interest and property tax payments. For another, the equity you build up as you pay for your home will probably represent a sizable nest egg by the time you're ready to sell. And with the traditionally upward trend in real estate prices, you'll probably find that the value of your home has increased substantially during your period of ownership.

But what if you can't afford to buy your own home? What if you prefer to live in an apartment, where the building is maintained and repaired by others with a minimum of headaches for you? Or what if there are few or no affordable homes in the areas where you want to live? For any or all of these reasons, you may want to consider buying a condominium or cooperative apartment as an alternative to home ownership.

What Is a Condominium?

A *condominium*, or *condo*, is an arrangement in which you own your own dwelling unit, usually an apartment but sometimes an individual house, row house, duplex, or other unit. Therefore, you have the same control over your property as does the owner of a conventional house. However, you also own a share in the common properties used by all the owners in a particular building or complex, including the land, the lobby, the heating and electrical system, and the parking lots, as well as any community facilities such as a golf course, recreation hall, or swimming pool. In these areas you do not have full control. Control (including maintenance) of the land and amenities (pool, tennis court, etc.) lies in the hands of the owners' association, and your input into the decisions of the association is limited to the size of your shareholdings. You must pay a monthly maintenance fee to the developer of the condominium; this fee covers your share of the operating costs. In addition, you must pay your own property taxes and any mortgage you need to buy the apartment, just as most homeowners do.

Since you are the owner of your own condominium unit, the finances of condominium ownership resemble those of buying a house. You must arrange for your own financing, generally by taking out a mortgage from the bank or other financial institution. Mortgage money for condominiums is usually readily available, sometimes at interest rates slightly lower than those charged for home mortgages. The portion of your mortgage payments devoted to interest payment is deductible from your income prior to federal taxation—a substantial benefit for condominium owners. Your property tax payments, too, are deductible from your income for federal tax purposes. And since you own your condominium unit, you can sell it when you like to whomever you wish. If the value of the property has grown, you can walk away with a tidy profit.

What Are the Advantages and Disadvantages of Condominium Ownership?

As you can see, condominium ownership can offer some important benefits. Here are some of the other advantages of owning a condo unit:

- It usually costs less to buy a condominium than to buy a private home, and, as already mentioned, condo financing is often easier to arrange.

- Condominium projects are professionally maintained, which can alleviate much of the anxiety of owning your own home. This can be especially important for the elderly, who may want to escape chores such as painting, shoveling snow, and trimming hedges.

- Safety and security are usually tighter in a multiple dwelling such as a condo apartment complex than in an isolated private home—another important consideration for older people in particular.

- Finally, the sharing of costs among a large group of owners permits luxuries individual homeowners usually can't afford—swimming pools, tennis courts, clubhouses, and the like.

This is not to say that condo ownership is without drawbacks or pitfalls. Here are some cautionary notes to consider before making a condo purchase:

- When investigating a particular condominium project, check the quality and condition of the property carefully.

Make sure the plumbing, electrical, and heating systems are in good working order. The developer should be willing to certify the condition of the structure. If the condominium is in a newly built development, don't rely on assurances that special facilities, such as a pool or golf course, will "soon be available." If these amenities aren't in place and operating when you buy, you may never see them.

- When you own a condo, all decisions concerning the common properties of the condominium project are made by a management committee and ratified by a vote of the individual owners. The weight of your vote depends on the size of your unit: the bigger your apartment, the more votes you'll have. Nonetheless, the wishes of the majority of owners will normally prevail. Can this become a problem? Yes, if decisions are made which affect living conditions at the condo in ways you don't approve—the prohibition of pets, for example.

- The maintenance fee you pay is not permanently fixed, as it may increase because of ordinary price inflation. It may also have to be boosted if the maintenance budget initially set by the developer was unrealistically low. This is something to consider carefully before buying.

- When you wish to sell your condo, you don't need the permission of the management committee. However, the committee often has the right of first refusal on your property, and so may require early notification of your intention to sell.

What Is Needed in Order to Own a Condo?

Every investment involves much paperwork, and you must be extremely careful to understand the many documents needed in condo ownership.

1. The declaration or master deed will describe the physical details of your condo ownership. This deed contains the conditions and restrictions of ownership.

2. The condo association's bylaws are also an important document for you to examine. These bylaws contain all the rules and regulations of the condo.

3. The condo management agreement (if the project is managed by a professional management company) will disclose who operates the condo, the duties of the managers, and the rates charged by the management company.

4. The title insurance commitment, or an abstract certified to date, will disclose whether the seller has clear title to the condo (free of any mortgages or liens). This document is essential when you are contemplating the purchase of a condo.

5. The purchase agreement (offer) is the most important document in your condo transactions because once it is signed by you and accepted by the seller, it will govern every aspect of the purchase, including condition of the property, repairs to be made, construction of amenities, and simple things such as color of paint, fixtures to be included, and appliances. Verbal descriptions are not binding, so any representations must be in writing. Therefore, you should employ experienced counsel well in advance of signing any papers.

Condo ownership can be ideal for many people. But make sure you understand the terms of the arrangement before you get involved. See that the maintenance fees are spelled out, read the rules and restrictions carefully, and have the condition of the property checked out thoroughly. Above all, be sure you're dealing with an established, reputable developer. Talk to friends, call the local Better Business Bureau, and ask at your bank. If anything you hear makes you doubt the reliability of the seller, back off.

What Is a Cooperative?

A *cooperative*, or *co-op*, differs from a condominium in several ways. When you buy a co-op, you buy a share or a number of shares in the corporation that owns and manages the land and the buildings. These shares entitle you to occupy a particular apartment for a specified term. However, you do not own the apartment, as you would when buying a condo. As a co-op owner, you must pay a monthly maintenance fee, which includes not only your share of the cost of maintaining the building and grounds (like the condo maintenance fee) but also your share of the mortgage costs and taxes on the entire property, which are paid by the corporation as a whole. Note that you can deduct from your income, for tax purposes, the portion of your monthly maintenance fee which goes to pay for interest on the corporate mortgage and property taxes. In addition, of course, you may have to make payments on the mortgage loan you took out to purchase your shares in the co-op. If you get a co-op loan, unlike a condo loan, you will not have to pay a mortgage recording tax because buying a co-op is not considered a real estate investment but is deemed ownership of shares in a corporation. It is also easier to get a co-op loan because a title search is not required under co-op ownership.

What Other Differences Should the Investor Know Of?

There are other differences between a condo and a co-op. When decisions affecting the management of the development must be made, condo owners have voting power weighted according to the size of the units they own. A co-op owner has a single vote, per share, regardless of the size of the apartment he or she may own. A condo owner may sell the unit to anyone (although the management usually has the first right of refusal). By contrast, the corporation which manages the co-op has complete control over the buying and selling of apartments. You may be required to sell your apartment only to the corporation; you will certainly have to obtain permission before you can sell it to anyone else. And the corporation will probably also have to approve any major alterations you wish to make in your apartment. However, as with a condo, any appreciation in the value of your co-op apartment during your period of ownership will benefit you when the time comes to sell.

The strict control over the property held by a co-op's management can be both an advantage and a disadvantage to the individual owner. On the one hand, it restricts your freedom to do as you like with the apartment. On the other hand, as a voting shareholder in the corporation, you may like the idea that the corporation can limit and control the uses to which the property is put and, to some extent, the people who move in. In fact, this feature of the co-op has been used by many wealthy people as a way of preventing those whom they consider "undesirable" from becoming their neighbors. If you're a typical middle-class person, this feature will probably not have much appeal to you.

There is one more important difference between condo and co-op ownership. When you buy shares in a co-op, you are investing in a corporation, and, in effect, becoming business partners with the other co-op owners. This means that you can be held responsible for the solvency of the enterprise. And if a co-op owner defaults on his or her maintenance payments, you and the other co-op owners will have to help make up the difference. Therefore, the reliability of those buying shares in the co-op should be an important consideration in deciding whether or not to get involved. That is the reason why lenders such as banks usually charge more for a co-op loan than for a condo loan. This extra potential liability adds to the charges. In contrast, condo ownership means responsibility for your own unit only, and a default on a condo loan cannot be passed on to other condo owners.

On balance, the condominium is probably a more favorable choice for most people than the co-op. However, if you're an apartment renter, you may find one day that the owner of your building has decided to "go co-op," that is, to attempt to convert the building from rentals to co-ops, with the former owner as the manager of the newly formed corporation. If this happens, you will, of course, be faced with the decision of whether or not to purchase shares in the co-op. If you decide that you do wish to purchase, on the basis of your financial situation and how well you like your apartment, fine. If for some reason you prefer not to join the co-op, you should be aware of the rights you have as a renter in a building going co-op. It is impossible to list these rights here, as they will vary from one state and city to another, because of local laws, but you can find out about them by contacting any local realtor.

As you can see, either a condominium or a co-op can be a worthwhile investment. Both provide tax advantages that renting cannot offer, and with both arrangements you own a property (either the actual dwelling unit or a share in the co-op) which has a good chance of growing in value while you use it. Therefore, if you're currently renting the home in which you live and buying a house is either impractical or just not your cup of tea, look into the local condo and co-op markets. Both are options well worth considering. And on the topic of real estate, for what I paid for my townhouse today, 100 years ago I could have bought the town.

5

Corporate Bond Market— For the Future

If a company can't pay as it goes, it may be going too fast.

Although bonds have become popular with many investors, they are still widely misunderstood. There are many kinds of bonds, and investing in them wisely can be a complex, challenging task. However, the rewards are often great, and bonds are an option well worth investigating for the middle-income investor.

How Do Corporate Bonds Work?

A *bond* is a form of debt issued by a government or a corporation. In exchange for a sum of money lent by the buyer of the bond, the issuer of the bond promises to pay a specific amount of interest at stated intervals for a specific period of time. At the end of the repayment period (that is, at maturity), the issuer repays the amount of money borrowed. You can read about the bonds issued by state and federal governments elsewhere in this book (Chapters 12 and 18). In this section we'll discuss the special characteristics of corporate bonds—those issued by corporations.

The holder of a corporate bond is a creditor of the corporation which issues the bond, not a part owner like a stockholder. Therefore, if the corporation's profits increase during the term of the bond, the bondholder will not benefit; the amount of interest he or she receives is fixed at the time the bond is purchased. On the other hand, the bondholder's investment is safer than that of the stockholder. Interest on bonds is paid out before dividends are distributed to stockholders. Furthermore, if the corporation goes bankrupt, the claims of bondholders take precedence over those of stockholders.

Newly issued corporate bonds are usually sold by a brokerage firm, which acts as underwriter of the issue. The underwriter receives the bonds from the issuing corporation and guarantees the corporation a specified level of sales, and then sells the bonds to the public. This is known as the *primary* bond market.

There is also a secondary bond market. It also operates through brokerage firms. The secondary market deals in previously issued bonds, which, as you'll see, may have either increased or decreased in value since their initial offering.

What Are the Characteristics of Bonds?

Some bonds are issued with property (such as land, buildings, machinery, or other equipment) as collateral against the loan, just as you might offer collateral to a bank in exchange for a personal loan. These bonds are known as *secured bonds*. Bonds not secured by collateral are called *debentures*. The value of a debenture is guaranteed by the good faith of the corporation, and if issued by a strong corporation, the debenture can be a highly secure investment.

All bonds bear both a face value and a maturity date. The face value is the amount you normally must spend to buy the bond when it is issued; it represents the amount of money you are lending the issuing corporation. The maturity date is when the face value of the bond must be repaid. Thus a 20-year bond issued in 1992 must be repaid in full in 2012.

Interest on corporate bonds is usually paid in one of two ways. *Coupon bonds,* also called *bearer bonds,* have interest coupons attached to them. You clip the coupons as they become due and present them for payment of interest. Your name usually doesn't appear on a coupon bond; it is a negotiable instrument, and anyone who clips the coupons can claim the interest due. However, this type of bond is no longer issued but it may be available in the secondary marketplace. By contrast, a *registered bond* bears its owner's name and can be transferred from one owner to another only by the endorsement of the registered owner. Interest on a registered bond is paid through the mail by check.

Corporate bonds are usually issued in denominations of $1000. After issue, however, their prices vary. A bond's *par value* is $1000, and its value at any given time is quoted as a percentage of par. Thus a bond quoted at 100 is selling at 100 percent of par, or $1000. If the price is quoted at 95, it is selling at 95 percent of par; you could buy such a bond for $950. This is known as a *discounted bond.* A *premium bond* is one which sells at a price higher than par. A bond with a quoted price of 102, for example, will cost $1020, which is 102 percent of par.

Why does the price of a corporate bond fluctuate? This is because of the fixed rate paid by the bond. As the current market interest rate increases, the relative value of the fixed rate paid by a bond decreases and so does the price of the bond. When the current market interest rate decreases, the fixed rate paid by the bond becomes increasingly attractive, and the value of the bond goes up as a result.

What Are the Different Types of Bonds?

There are many variations in the types of bonds issued by corporations. You should understand some of the most important ones.

A bond may be issued with a *callability* clause. A callable bond may be redeemed by the issuing corporation prior to the maturity date; that is, the corporation may, at its option, call in the bonds early and repay them at that time (though usually at a premium over the face value). The corporation is likely to exercise this option when market interest rates have fallen below those in effect at the time the bond was issued. If new market conditions call for interest rates of 10 percent, why should a corporation continue to pay 12 or 14 percent on its previously issued bonds? As you can see, callability is a drawback for investors, since it prevents them from locking in high interest rates. For this reason, callable bonds usually pay a higher interest rate than comparable noncallable bonds.

All bonds issued since July 1983 must be registered. This means that the issuer of the bonds records the purchase and sends out the interest checks. If the bonds are registered in your name, the issuer will notify you of the call. If the bonds are registered in the street-name account held by your broker, the broker will be notified of the call and in turn will notify you. For bonds issued before July 1983 that were not registered (coupon bonds), it is the bondholder's responsibility to find out about the call.

Recently, a few corporations have begun to offer protection for a specified period against the possibility of a bond being called. The "call protection" usually runs 5 to 10 years, and it guarantees the bondholder a specific interest rate for at least a minimum number of years. Always check the call provision in any bond contract you are considering.

Some corporations issue *convertible bonds,* which may be exchanged for shares of the corporation's common stock at the option of the bondholder. This can allow you to participate in a greater-than-expected growth in the profits and value of the corporation. Convertible bonds thus combine the stability and safety of bonds with the growth opportunity of common stock. If you believe a company will move upward but you are concerned about the ups and downs over the short term, the convertible bond would be a good investment for you. If the common stock value goes down, the convertible bond keeps its fixed yield. But when the common stock rises, you might want to sell the bond and take advantage of the gain. For example, a company with common stock trading at $20 per share might issue a $1000 convertible bond that pays 9 percent interest and is exchangeable for 40 shares of common stock ($25 per share). The bondholder would not convert at the present time to shares because he or she would be able to buy those same 40 shares at $800 in the current market. But if the shares increased in value to more than $25 per share, he or she could convert the bonds to shares, sell the shares, and make a profit. Until a decision is made to convert, the bond will pay $90 per year in interest. As usual, however, there's no free ride: You must ordinarily sacrifice about 1 percentage point in interest yield in exchange for the convertibility feature. The important feature is that there is a limited down-side risk but virtually a limitless up-side potential.

What Factors Should You Consider When Purchasing Bonds?

There are two principal factors to weigh in considering the purchase of a particular corporate bond: (1) the yield offered by the bond and (2) the safety of the investment. Let's consider each of these factors in some detail.

What Is Yield as Applied to Bonds?

With regard to bonds, the very term *yield* can be confusing. There are several types of yields associated with bonds.

The *coupon yield*, or *coupon rate*, is the interest rate stated on the bond itself.

The *actual yield* is the ratio of return that the coupon yield actually produces when the cost of the bond is taken into account. If you purchase the bond above par, the actual yield is lower than the coupon yield; if you purchase the bond below par, the actual yield is higher. For example, a $1000 bond with an 8 percent coupon rate bought at 82 (for a cost of $820) would produce an actual yield of 9.7 percent (8 percent of $1000, or $80, ÷ $820). The same bond bought at 104 (for a cost of $1040) would actually yield only 7.7 percent ($80 ÷ $1040).

The *current yield* is the actual yield based on the closing price of the bond on the bond market for a given day. When the price of the bond declines, the current yield increases; when the price of the bond increases, the current yield declines. For example, suppose a $1000 bond with an 8 percent coupon rate closed on the trading market on Friday at $910. The current yield for the bond on Friday would be 8.8 percent ($80 ÷ $910).

Finally, *yield to maturity* represents the total rate of return if the bond is held to maturity, taking into consideration the purchase price of the bond, the interest paid, and the redemption price. Any broker can refer to a standard reference book which contains yield-to-maturity figures for almost any conceivable bond.

Naturally, all things being equal, the higher the yield on a particular bond, the better buy that bond is likely to be. But all things are not always equal. Bonds also differ in their degree of safety. That brings us to the second dominant consideration in choosing a bond for purchase.

What Is Safety as Applied to Bonds?

The degree of risk associated with the purchase of a particular bond depends on the strength of the issuing corporation. Of course, it's not easy for the average middle-income investor to analyze the performance of all the many bond-issuing corporations. For a full examination, it would be necessary to study the company's financial statements, its earnings projections, the track record of management, prospects for the industry, and many other factors.

Fortunately, you don't need to do all this research yourself. There are special advisory services which have assumed the task of analyzing and rating the safety of corporate bonds. These ratings can be obtained from reference books you can readily find at your public library or request from any brokerage house.

The two best-known rating services are Moody's and Standard & Poor's (S&P). They rate bonds according to two slightly differing scales. Starting with the highest-rated bonds, the two scales are as follows:

Moody's: Aaa, Aa, A, Baa, Ba, B, Caa, Ca, C

S&P: AAA, AA, A, BBB, BB, B, CCC, CC, C

The most risk-free bonds—those issued by large, stable corporations showing excellent future earnings projections—are rated Aaa or AAA. Bonds rated AA or A are issued by firms whose ability to pay interest and principal is quite strong, but the safety of these bonds is somewhat more vulnerable to changes in economic conditions.

As you move toward the lower end of the rating scale, yields are likely to be higher; the lower-rated firms must offer higher interest rates to induce investors to accept the greater degree of risk. The bonds on the lowest rungs of the ladder are sometimes called "junk bonds." These bonds have ratings of BB or lower and usually pay yields about 3 percentage points higher than A-rated bonds. They received their disparaging nickname in the late 1920s and early 1930s, when the Great Depression led to numerous defaults by bond issuers, and are today considered one of the major factors in the savings and loan failures and the inadequate financing of major mergers and acquisitions. The junk bonds offer neither the security of bonds nor the growth of stocks. There are those who will argue that junk bonds have done well in the past. Perhaps a statement I heard about them will suffice. If you ask a drunk at 11 p.m. how he feels, the answer is "fine." The big question is, how will the drunk feel in the morning?

Most brokers will quote the standard bond ratings along with prices and yields when you inquire about possible investments. For maximum safety, you'll probably want to stick to bonds rated A and higher. However, even though a bond may have an AA rating when you purchase it, that rating is always subject to change, upward or downward. The only exception would be if you want to choose a low-rated, high-yielding bond on a speculative basis. If you do, make sure that the amount you risk in this way is no greater than the amount you can afford to lose. Greed—especially for the ill-informed investor—can lead to devastating mistakes.

How Do You Learn about Bonds?

If you're interested in getting into the bond market, you should know how to read the bond quotations which appear on the business page of your daily newspaper. These are a good basic source of information about currently available bonds. Figure 5.1 provides a sample bond listing as it might

Issue	Descrip- tion	Current Yield	Volume	High	Low	Last	Change
ABC	8¾ 02	9.8	28	90	88½	89	+2

Issue: The abbreviated name of the corporation issuing the bond; in this case, ABC.

Description: A description of the bond. This bond has a coupon yield of 8¾ percent and matures in 2002.

Current Yield: The annual interest on a $1000 bond divided by today's closing price for the bond. In this case, 8¾ percent of $1000 ($87.50) divided by $890 = 9.8 percent.

Volume: The number of $1000 bonds traded that day.

High: The highest price of the day; in this case, 90 percent of par, or $900 for a $1000 bond.

Low: The lowest price of the day; in this case, 88½ percent of par, or $885 for a $1000 bond.

Last: The day's closing price; in this case, 89 percent of par, or $890 for a $1000 bond.

Change: The difference between today's closing price and yesterday's. Since today's closing price of $890 is 2 points higher than yesterday's, yesterday's closing price must have been 87, or $870.

Figure 5.1 Sample corporate bond listing.

appear in the newspaper. You'll find an explanation of the information each column provides below the sample listing.

Bonds make an excellent choice for many middle-income investors, especially those whose primary need is for income rather than growth. Older people looking toward retirement, for example, are likely to find bonds a particularly attractive investment. However, since bonds are available in so many different forms, be careful in your selections. Remember the importance of safety, and use the standard ratings as your guide. And be sure you understand the details of the particular bond issue you are considering before you buy. The informed investor can do very well in today's corporate bond market. And on the topic of information, education is what you get when you read the fine print; experience is what you get when you don't.

6

Ginnie Mae— The Misunderstood Instrument

Some think that Ginnie Mae is just a little
girl and that Fannie Mae is her mother.

If I had to choose the most misunderstood financial instrument from among the many about which I write, I would pick the government-insured mortgage.

What Is a Ginnie Mae?

The Government National Mortgage Association (GNMA) was formed by Congress in 1968 as a branch of the Department of Housing and Urban Development. Its objective was to buy government-insured mortgages, similar to those guaranteed by the Federal Housing Administration (FHA) and the Veterans Administration (VA), from the banks which originally made the loans. By doing this, the GNMA provides the lending institutions with the money to offer additional mortgages.

After buying these FHA and VA mortgages, the GNMA

groups them into units of a million dollars or more, known as *pools*. These pools are then sold to investment brokerage houses, with an additional guarantee against default added by GNMA. The brokers, in turn, sell shares in these units of $25,000 or more. These shares are known as *Ginnie Mae pass-through certificates*. The name "Ginnie Mae" is a fanciful pronunciation of GNMA, and the term *pass-through certificate* comes from the fact that, when an investor buys the certificate, the homeowner's mortgage payments are passed through to the investor.

How Does the Ginnie Mae Work?

To explain how the Ginnie Mae works, let's follow one mortgage as it is created with the borrower and ultimately winds up in the hands of the investor. Mr. J takes out an FHA mortgage with the Penny National Bank. This bank combines about 50 other similar mortgages totaling approximately $1 million, and sells these mortgages to the GNMA. This gives the Penny Bank its funds back so that it can lend more money again. The GNMA can either retain this pool of mortgages or sell it to investors. A brokerage house may purchase the pool, carve it up into smaller units, and sell them to its clients, the general public. It then moves out of the picture, leaving the original lender collecting Mr. J's monthly payment and forwarding it to the investing public who just bought the Ginnie Mae. If Mr. J should not be able to meet his mortgage payments, the bank will foreclose and the government will make good that portion of the default.

As you can see, the Ginnie Mae is a way of investing in a large pool of government-guaranteed mortgages simply by purchasing a share in the pool. Since the smallest units sold are $25,000 packages, institutional investors do most of the direct trading in Ginnie Maes. However, it's possible to get involved in Ginnie Maes for as little as $1000 by buying a unit in a Ginnie Mae mutual fund or trust.

Are Ginnie Maes Safe?

Ginnie Maes are an excellent, safe investment. Because of the involvement of the GNMA, payments of both principal and interest on the mortgage loans are fully guaranteed by the federal government. This guarantee is in addition to the government guarantee which already covers FHA and VA mortgages, so the degree of risk in Ginnie Maes is as small as you're ever likely to get. However, they are not considered obligations of the United States and are therefore subject to federal, state, and any local taxes.

I know that it sounds confusing when the law reads that "states are not permitted to tax obligations of the United States" and yet everyone considers Ginnie Maes obligations of the United States. Well, yes and no. The first obligation to make payment on Ginnie Maes rests with the financial institution that issues the certificates. The U.S. government is only a guarantor in the unlikely event of default.

How Is Income Paid to the Investor?

Income from Ginnie Maes is paid on a monthly basis. If you own a Ginnie Mae, you'll receive (around the fifteenth of each month) a check representing an installment of the repayment of the mortgages in the pool into which you've bought. A part of each check represents repayment of the principal on the loan; the rest is interest. An enclosed statement will tell you what portion of the check is interest and what portion is principal—something you'll need to know, since the interest portion is taxable while the principal payments are not. During the early months of the repayment period, you'll mainly receive interest; later payments include a higher percentage of principal. This may be advantageous at times, but it might present a problem. The continual return of your principal can expose you to what is known as *reinvestment risk*. Normally, during falling interest rates, your payments accelerate, meaning that you will get money that will be reinvested at lower rates. Also, some people tend to forget that, with each month's payment, they receive, included in the total amount, a portion of their principal. Many times this is ignored and the total amount is spent as if it were all interest. Remember that when those checks stop coming, there is no principal left.

There is a variation of this system by which you can arrange to have the principal remain intact and receive only interest payments. Younger investors may wish to consider this option since it provides for steady payments of interest on a fixed principal, which itself is paid in full at the time when the certificate matures. Older investors—retirees, for example—will probably prefer the usual interest-plus-principal repayment plan, since they generally have a greater need for monthly income than for a large lump-sum payment at the end.

There is one major drawback to investing in Ginnie Maes— the impossibility of predicting their yield. The monthly checks you'll receive will vary in size, and the period over which the checks keep coming may vary also. The reason is that no one is certain when the mortgages will be paid in full. As you know, some people take a full 30 years to repay their mortgage loans; others sell their houses and repay the mortgages after only a year or two. Since no one can predict how long the homeowners in a particular pool will take to repay their loans, no one can predict exactly how long the payments will last or how large each monthly payment will be. Therefore, one month you might receive a large check that is an unexpected payoff of principal, but then subsequent checks might be smaller, because you will be earning the same rate on a smaller principal. If you place your money in the Federal National Mortgage Association (FNMA) or the Federal Home Loan Mortgage Corporation (FHLMC) (see Chapter 7), you will be involved in at least 1000 mortgages rather than the GNMA's 50. Therefore, the impact of early payback is greatly diminished.

To find the best "deal" from your broker, look for a seasoned pool that has a history of stability. Watch out for any pool based on mortgages with single-digit interest rates because with those low rates, homeowners will usually stay with the mortgage until the end (sometimes as long as 30 years). Such a pool will pay out longer than the 12-year average, which will tie up your money and produce even lower returns than you had anticipated.

When Does the Ginnie Mae Mature?

One rule of thumb brokers often cite is that Ginnie Mae mortgage pools are repaid, on the average, within 12 years. This means that if you buy a Ginnie Mae certificate, you can estimate that you'll continue to receive monthly checks for about 12 years; and those checks will be larger in the beginning than near the end, since the amount of outstanding debt will be greater at that time. Neither prediction is guaranteed. For example, your certificate may continue to pay monthly checks for 15 years or more, or it may be entirely paid out within 5 to 8 years or less. Bear in mind that the Ginnie Mae is not a financial instrument to speculate with for a short period of time. When you purchase one, you are not involved with "Ginnie" for a quickie romance; you are in for a long-term relationship. The reason is that the bid/ask spread on this instrument (the difference between what is paid for the instrument and its selling price) is very costly and you could lose a great deal on a short-term basis. It would probably be more beneficial if you bought a Ginnie Mae mutual fund (see the last section of this chapter) even if it costs you about a half point in lower yields. At least you will have the confidence of knowing that you can get out at any time.

How Do Current Interest Rates Affect the Ginnie Mae?

Changes in the market interest rate on mortgages play an important role here. The interest rate you'll receive on your Ginnie Mae depends, of course, on the mortgage rate at the time the pool was established. If mortgage rates fall below that figure, it's likely that repayment of your Ginnie Mae will be accelerated. This is because the homeowners who took out the mortgages will be eager to repay their high-interest loans and refinance their homes at the new, lower rates. So, you'll get back your money sooner and be forced to reinvest it elsewhere at the new, lower prevailing interest rates. For example, the 1981 high-interest-rate Ginnie Maes (15 to 17 percent) will certainly be turned in, as any homeowner with huge debt service would refinance at the earliest opportunity.

By contrast, if mortgage interest rates rise, the life of your Ginnie Mae is likely to be prolonged. Homeowners will be content to keep paying the relatively low rate of interest they locked in at the time they took out their mortgages, and you'll continue to receive checks for longer than the average 12-year repayment period.

As you can see, Ginnie Maes are not an ideal investment for those who must be able to predict their future monthly income with absolute certainty. If you can afford to be flexible, you can afford to consider Ginnie Maes.

There is a major secondary market in Ginnie Maes made up of shares in mortgage pools established at some time in the past. Like previously issued bonds, previously issued Ginnie Maes fluctuate in value owing to market conditions. Depending on the age of the certificate, the number of monthly payments that have already been made, and interest rate considerations, you may be able to buy an older Ginnie Mae certificate at a considerable discount from its face value. A Ginnie Mae quoted at 90 sells for 90 percent of its face value; that is, a $25,000 certificate would cost $22,500.

If you are concerned about taking a loss when selling your Ginnie Mae, consider the following. If the certificate is sold prior to maturity and interest rates rise, your Ginnie Mae would be sold at a loss because it is a fixed-rate instrument. You can avoid any fluctuations by purchasing a Ginnie Mae certificate backed by an adjustable-rate mortgage (ARM) pool. Since the rate of interest is adjusted on the certificate, the Ginnie Mae should trade at close to its original price.

What Other Factors Should You Know About?

In addition to the quoted price there are two important factors to consider when you look at previously issued Ginnie Maes: the *pool factor* and the *pool speed*.

The pool factor is the percentage of the principal that remains unpaid in a particular mortgage pool. The higher the pool factor, the longer it will probably take for the loan repayments to be completed and the longer you will continue to receive checks. The pool speed is the relative speed with which repayment of loans in a particular pool is occurring. This will vary depending on economic conditions, the interest rate at the time the pool was established, and the geographic areas in which the mortgages were issued. If the pool speed is high, your Ginnie Mae checks will probably end fairly soon; if the pool speed is low, they will probably last longer.

Therefore, you can readily understand that for the following reasons, the Ginnie Mae is an investment worth looking into.

1. Your money is backed by the U.S. government even if the borrowers do not meet their obligations.

2. The loans are liquid and may be resold if necessary.

3. There is a monthly cash flow that allows debt repayment to go from borrower to bank, which will then service you, the investor.

4. You can reinvest your monthly income during periods of higher interest rates.

5. The yields are attractive and higher than Treasury obligations. Also, because mortgages compound every month rather than every 6 months, as with bonds, the yield is higher than what is stated.

How Can the Small Investor Purchase a Ginnie Mae?

Many people can't afford the $25,000 minimum investment required to buy a Ginnie Mae certificate. If you're one of these people, consider buying a unit in a Ginnie Mae mutual or trust fund. These units usually sell for $1000, and can be bought and sold through brokers. Each fund has its own rules and procedures, as well as its own portfolio of mortgage holdings, which may affect the income you'll receive. When you invest in a Ginnie Mae fund, you may have to pay a sales charge of up to 3.5 percent. There may be instead, or in addition, an annual service or management fee. As with any mutual fund, shop around and ask questions before writing a check. And on the topic of questions, the only things worth learning are the things you learn after you know it all.

7

Ginnie Mae Alternatives

The hardest lesson to learn in life to decide
which bridges to cross and which to burn.

When you investigate Ginnie Maes, you may hear references to two other forms of mortgage-backed securities: Freddie Macs and Fannie Maes. Freddie Macs are issued by the Federal Home Loan Mortgage Corporation (FHLMC) and focus on conventional loans which it purchases in quantity and then resells. A minimum of $25,000 is needed to invest in Freddie Mac *participation certificates* (PCs). The mortgages in the Freddie Mac pools are usually not government-insured loans, like the FHA and VA mortgages in which the GNMA specializes, but are privately issued, nonguaranteed mortgages. As a consequence, the FHLMC does not absolutely guarantee your investment as the GNMA does; instead, you are guaranteed "timely" payments of interest and "ultimate" repayment of principal. It's possible, then, that you might be kept waiting for some of your money when you invest in a Freddie Mac. As with most forms of investment, the slightly greater risk with a Freddie Mac is counterbalanced by a higher rate of return—usually ¼ to ½ percent or more. Note also that the market for Freddie Macs is much smaller than that for Ginnie Maes, so it might take a while to liquidate your holdings if and when you decide to sell.

How Do Fannie Maes and Freddie Macs Work?

Fannie Maes are issued by the Federal National Mortgage Association (FNMA). The FNMA serves the secondary mortgage market by buying single and multifamily loans and then reselling them to investors by way of mortgage-backed securities. In most ways, Fannie Maes are similar to Freddie Macs, and, as with Ginnie Maes, timely payments of both interest and principal are guaranteed. Unlike Ginnie Maes, which consist of mortgages insured by the FHA or guaranteed by the VA, Fannie Maes may include either government-backed loans or privately insured conventionals. In the latter case, the FNMA (rather than the government) stands behind the debt. Do not overly concern yourself about the safety of either the FNMA or the FHLMC, as both organizations are government-chartered companies, and their issues are considered to be "moral obligations" of the government. They also yield slightly higher interest rates than the GNMA.

The risk faced by an investor in Ginnie Maes, Fannie Maes, or Freddie Macs is not that the homeowners will not make their monthly payments, but just the opposite, that they might pay off their mortgages too rapidly if mortgage rates should fall. This can occur when homeowners sell, refinance, or exchange a high-interest mortgage for a lower-interest one. The trouble for the investor is that there is a sudden infusion of money because a prepayment by a homeowner will cause all interest payments on the mortgage to stop, and this repaid principal will then have to be reinvested, usually at a lower rate. This early payment problem can now be overcome with the introduction of the *collateralized mortgage obligation* (CMO).

How Does the CMO Work?

The CMO works in the same fashion as the Ginnie Mae. However, the CMO takes the cash flows from many mortgage-backed securities and splits them into groups of bonds with different maturities instead of a single maturity, as with the Ginnie Mae. It could be said that the CMO can be broken down into three time period groups: (1) fast pay, (2) medium pay, and (3) slow pay. As with ordinary bonds, most CMOs pay interest twice a year. However, principal repayments will go first to the classes with the shortest maturity. When they are retired, the principal will then go to the bonds with the next shortest maturity, and so on, until all classes have been paid off. There could be as many as a dozen different classes (known as *tranches*) of maturity. Instead of one security with a final stated maturity of 20 years, there would be many different classes of maturities (3 years, 5 years, 9 years, etc.). In other words, those holding the "fast pay" will get a portion of the mortgage interest payments and receive all the prepayments on the underlying mortgages until everyone in that group has been fully repaid (2 to 3 years). If investors want higher returns (usually ½ percent) they can choose the "slow pay" option. Under this option the investor will receive interest for several years (10 to 20 years) but will get no principal until all the shorter-term bonds have been repaid. At that time, payments may continue.

Because the CMO does not have a single retirement date, it is a vast improvement over the Ginnie Mae, which begins to pay off principal the month that it is issued. CMOs are designed to meet different maturity needs and are thus more attractive to investors than traditional mortgage pass-throughs.

How Do You Buy CMOs?

CMOs are issued in book entry form and are subject to federal and state income tax on their coupon income. CMOs are quoted as a percentage of face value. A $1000 bond, quoted at a price of 99, would cost $990. This will include a commission of ½ to 3 percent depending on the length of maturity (the longer the period, the higher the commission). Don't buy a CMO priced more than a full point below face value because if interest rates rise, your projected length of maturity can be much longer than expected since fewer people will refinance. In essence, you will have a low-yielding investment for a long term. On the other hand, don't purchase a CMO priced more than a full point above par because if interest rates should fall, your premium will disappear and the high rate of return will not be with you for any lengthy period of time because of high prepayments. Bear in mind also that although CMOs can be sold at any time, they are meant to be held until maturity.

How Safe Are CMOs?

CMOs are backed either by the GNMA, FNMA, or FHLMC, or by private insurance. Ratings are not based on the credit of the issuer but instead on the quantity and quality of the underlying collateral. CMOs issued directly by the FNMA and FHLMC are backed by securities which are guaranteed by those agencies. CMOs backed by agency pass-throughs are rated AAA by Standard & Poor's or Moody's, whereas those backed by private mortgage insurance are often rated AA. And on the topic of safety, although wearing a suit of armor protects you from harm, it also keeps you from pleasure.

8

Gold, Silver, and Diamonds— Investment or Enjoyment?

The golden rule: whoever has the gold rules.

Gold has been used as money since biblical times. It has several characteristics that have made it desirable as a medium of exchange. Gold is scarce. It is durable. More than 95 percent of all the gold ever mined is still in circulation. And it is inherently valuable because of its beauty and its usefulness in industrial and decorative applications. Half a century ago the right to own gold bullion was taken away from the U.S. public, but that right was restored, in part, in 1975.

Why Is Gold Considered an Investment?

Gold has long been referred to as the "doomsday metal" because of its traditional role as a bulwark against economic, social, and political upheaval and the resulting loss of confidence in other investments, even those guaranteed by national governments. Yet this may not be true, as was seen during the stock market crash of 1987 and the terrible stock downturn in 1989, when the price of gold was expected to soar. As you may be aware, nothing occurred. When Iraq invaded Kuwait in 1990 and fighting began in 1991, the price of gold did not budge. Also, look at what happened when gold hit an all-time high of $825 on January 21, 1980, and then fell only 5 days later to $634 per ounce when people realized that the world wasn't coming to an end.

The value of gold changes daily, owing to economic and political conditions. When interest rates in the United States fall, the dollar grows weaker in relation to other currencies. As a result, foreign businesspeople find U.S. investment less attractive, and some of them turn to gold instead. This forces the price of gold higher. When interest rates in the United States rise, the reverse occurs.

Let me illustrate. It was wise in the 1970s to hold gold because high interest rates coupled with a high inflation rate could not provide a real rate of return. It is obvious that if you received an interest rate of 17 percent with an inflation rate of 16 percent, your true return would be only 1 percent. Therefore, gold became an investment as a store of value. But as the inflation rate dropped over the years, gold lost much of its appeal.

Why Is Gold Considered Risky?

The value of gold is volatile. Investing in gold carries with it a definite degree of risk. Any number of events which investors cannot control can influence the price of gold. Many government actions, such as a decision by the U.S. Treasury to sell some of its vast gold holdings, can cause a sharp drop in the price of gold. Even a soaring gold price can carry risks for the investor. If the price of gold becomes prohibitively high, industrial users of the metal may turn to substitutes. This could quickly increase the supply of gold relative to demand and so force the price down. On the other hand, gold could rise because of a sudden demand. For example, if a country has "too many dollars," it may in the near future become an active participant in buying gold.

There's one more drawback to investing in gold. Gold is a non-income-producing asset. That is, it earns profits only when it is sold for a price greater than its purchase price. Gold earns no interest while it sits in your vault. Therefore, gold should be purchased as an investment only by people who have no need of current income and who have time to watch the market and sell at an advantage. This is why gold has been compared to real estate—as an investment, it is easy to get into but difficult to leave. I personally feel that it takes a lot of "brass" to speculate in gold today.

Despite these drawbacks, gold can be considered a good investment for some. During its strong periods, gold has been known to increase in value many times over a short span of weeks or months. And, of course, gold has a strong aesthetic and emotional appeal. Unlike most other investments, gold can serve not only as a source of security for the future, but also as an ornament to be worn today.

What Do the Numbers Mean?

Pure gold is known as *24-karat* (24K) gold. In this form, it is too soft to be made into jewelry. Therefore, it is generally mixed with other metals, such as zinc, copper, nickel, and silver, for additional strength. The number of karats marked on an item of jewelry indicates the ratio of gold to other metals contained in the piece; the higher the karat rating, the more gold the item contains (and the higher its price is likely to be). For example, 18K gold contains 18 parts gold, 6 parts other metals; 14K gold contains 14 parts gold, 10 parts other metals. This means that 14K jewelry is only 58 percent gold.

What Are the Options for Investing in Gold?

See Table 8.1 for an overview of the types of gold investments discussed on pages 62 and 63.

TABLE 8.1. TYPES OF GOLD INVESTMENTS

	Bullion	Coins	Certificates	Shares and funds
Who should invest?	Conservative investors prepared to hold large amounts of gold for years	Conservative investors who wish to own small amounts of gold	Conservative investors, particularly those interested in buying at regular intervals	Aggressive investors
Where to purchase?	Large banks, coin dealers, stockbrokers	Most banks, stockbrokers, coin dealers	Brokers, large banks, and one dealer, Deak International	Stockbrokers, financial planners, by mail from no-load and low-load funds
What is the smallest investment?	Tiny bars weighing 1 gram (0.032 ounce); more typically, 1 ounce, 10 ounces, and 1 kilogram (32.15 ounces)	0.1-ounce coin, more typically 1 ounce	$250 in systematic buying programs that let you subsequently invest as little as $100 a month	The price of one share of an individual company; usually $250 in a mutual fund
Advantages	Low markup on large bars (2 to 3 percent)	Ease of buying and selling; portability	Low dealer markup (3 to 3.5 percent)	Maximum gains when gold prices rise; possible dividend income; no storage costs; diversification and professional management in funds; ease of buying and selling
Disadvantages	Cost of storage (usually in a bank vault) and insurance; cost of selling	Higher markup than on bars based on minting charges; cost of storage and insurance (about $7 a year for each coin)	Annual storage fee	Maximum losses when gold prices fall; risk of loss if a mine becomes unprofitable or because of political unrest (South Africa)

Gold bullion: When you buy gold bullion (that from Engelhard and from Johnson-Matthey is the most widely traded), you are buying gold in the form of bars that are 99.9 percent pure gold. You can actually take physical possession of the gold bars, or you can buy gold through a bank or broker that stores the gold in its own secure facilities. Although you can buy as little as an ounce of gold bullion, a minimum of 10 ounces is usually required, with a kilo bar (32.15 ounces) being the standard. When you buy gold bullion from metal brokers, you must pay certain charges (2 to 4 percent over the spot price) apart from the ounce-for-ounce value of the gold. In addition, some banks may charge a storage fee as high as 1 percent of its value per month for holding your gold. If you have gold bullion stored by a bank or broker, make certain that it is in a totally "nonfungible" storage program. This means that your gold is not combined with the assets of others but rather held separately and labeled with your name. Under such an arrangement, you have legal title to the gold, and it cannot be considered part of the assets of the bank or dealer which could be tied up by creditors in case of a liquidation.

Gold coins: Coins are a popular form for the purchase of gold. They are not only valuable but attractive, and since they are small and portable, they can be kept in a safe in your home or in any bank vault. Most gold coins are minted to weigh 1 ounce, but some weighing as little as $\frac{1}{10}$ ounce are available. Expect to pay between 4 and 17 percent beyond the value of the gold to cover the expense of minting and retail costs. Popular foreign gold coins include the Kruggerand, produced in South Africa (although new coins are presently banned for sale in the United States), the Corona (Australia), the Panda (China), the gold peso (Mexico), the Maple Leaf (Canada), and, of course, the American "Eagle." It is important to note that the Eagle is the only type of gold investment that may be used in an Individual Retirement Account (IRA).

Gold stocks: These are shares in companies whose business is gold mining. The purchase of gold stocks is a way of betting on the future price of gold without actually dealing in the metal itself. Gold stocks have some advantages over owning gold directly. Securities are more liquid than the metal, and no assaying or storage costs are involved. However, shares in gold-mining companies are "leveraged instruments." That is, the value of the stock is affected disproportionately by the value of the product being sold. When the value of gold rises, the value of the stock rises even faster, but when the value of gold falls, the value of gold stock falls faster and farther. In addition, most gold stocks pay no dividends, and when the gold originates in a foreign country, it may be subject to international risks. Stay away from gold mining stocks that purport to return riches quickly. If you want to "double your money," the safest way is to fold it and put it into your pocket!

Gold certificates: If you want to buy a small amount of gold (minimum around $2500) and do not want to take delivery, certain banks and brokers will allow you to make a purchase and receive a certificate of ownership rather than the gold itself. In essence, you are buying title to gold held at a bank or broker on your behalf. A yearly fee of about ½ percent is usually charged. The main advantage of this way of buying gold is that you do not need to have the gold assayed when you decide to sell it. This makes your assets more liquid.

As you can see, gold is not all "glitter," as it carries with it what is known as *opportunity cost*. This means that you have to give up current income that you would receive from any interest-producing asset. If this cost bothers you and you are more concerned with current income than with future gain, then gold is not the investment for you.

Is **silver** (the poor person's gold) a better investment as a precious metal? Where gold's primary role is monetary, silver's is industrial. Silver has many more commercial uses than gold—Kodak, for example, uses large amounts of silver every year in manufacturing photographic film—and because of its unique physical and chemical properties, no substitute for silver seems likely to be devised. These industrial uses provide a solid foundation for the future value of silver.

What Is the Relation between Gold and Silver?

The ratio of the price of gold to the price of silver is a useful investment guideline for those interested in buying either of these metals. You can easily determine the current gold/silver ratio by dividing the morning's gold price by that of silver. In past years, the average gold/silver ratio had been 32:1. A high or low gold/silver ratio indicates that one of the metals is currently undervalued in relation to the other, and you will want to consider moving your holdings into the undervalued metal. For example, a gold/silver ratio of 40:1 shows that silver is undervalued and therefore the metal to buy. A ratio of 15:1 means "buy gold."

How Do You Purchase Silver for Investment Purposes?

As with gold, there are several ways to buy silver. One way is to buy junk silver, which consists of a bag of pre-1965 U.S. dimes, quarters, or half dollars with a face value of $1000 and a market value based on the price of silver for the day. Silver bullion is available in 1000-ounce bars, while silver certificates are receipts for the purchase of silver, held at a bank in your name. Like gold certificates, silver certificates have the advantages of being highly liquid and posing no storage or security problems, so your wealth will remain intact.

A **diamond**, it has been said, is nothing more than a piece of coal that has made good under pressure. As an investment it has a great deal in common with gold. Both gold and diamonds tend to be costly in terms of brokers' fees and sales markups, but each offers the investor safety as a hedge against inflation. Diamonds are also a good hedge against depression. Have you noticed what happens when you give a diamond to a depressed spouse?

For people with substantial wealth who wish to concentrate a lot of that wealth in a small space, diamonds can be a sound investment. Unlike gold, diamonds don't demand continual monitoring of a highly volatile market; diamond prices don't fluctuate widely.

How Do You Purchase Diamonds?

If you do decide to buy diamonds for investment purposes, regard it as a long-term proposal, not a get-rich-quick scheme. Buy gems weighing from 1 to 3 carats and have them evaluated by an appraiser from the Gemological Institute of America (GIA). Once your diamond's GIA certificate is received, the stone's fair price can easily be determined by consulting a grading table since the certificate will state the "four C's": color, cut, clarity, and carat.

Color refers to how white or yellow a diamond is. The color of a diamond is rated alphabetically from D to Z. The closer a diamond is to the D grade, the whiter its color and the more valuable the stone. *Cut* refers to the shape of the diamond and the skill with which it has been crafted. The brilliance and beauty of a diamond depend largely on how accurately the diamond-cutter did his or her job. Note that round diamonds are generally the most stable. *Clarity* refers to the number and size of the flaws (or "inclusions") contained in the stone. It takes an expert with a magnifying glass to rate the clarity of a stone. Diamonds range from internally flawless (IF) to imperfect (I-3). *Carat* is the unit of weight for the gem, with 1 carat equaling 200 milligrams (1/142 ounce). The value of a diamond increases dramatically as its size increases; a 2-carat stone will usually be worth more than twice as much as a 1-carat stone of comparable quality.

What Are the Major Drawbacks to Investing in Diamonds?

1. Most diamonds appreciate in value less than 8 percent a year.

2. Like gold, diamonds are non-income-producing; no interest or dividends are paid on diamonds.

3. Diamonds are relatively difficult to liquidate.

4. The jewelry value of a diamond is much higher than its investment value because of heavy retail markups, which range from 40 to 300 percent, with 100 percent being the average. A diamond bought from a jeweler for $8000 is likely to yield only about $4000 if you decide to sell it to another jeweler later.

5. Storing and insuring diamonds are costly.

6. About 85 percent of the world's diamond market is controlled by the DeBeers-Central Selling Organization, headquartered in London. Therefore, the price of diamonds is dependent on the activities of a single group.

How Would You Summarize Investing in Precious Metals or Gems?

Gold, silver, and diamonds probably have more drawbacks than advantages as investment options for the average middle-income American. If you want to try your hand at investing in them, go ahead; if you have educated yourself and follow the market carefully, you may do very well. But most people will probably derive more benefit and happiness from the beauty and sentimental value of gold, silver, and diamond objects than they will from their investment value. And on the topic of happiness, the secret to being happy is to count your blessings while others are adding up their troubles.

9

Life Insurance—
The Risk Protector

For 3 days after death, hair and fingernails
continue to grow but phone calls do taper off.

What Is the Purpose of Life Insurance?

The basic purpose of life insurance is to offer financial protection to your loved ones in the event of your death. The benefit it provides is one you hope you won't need—at least not soon—but which most people would be foolish to do without. Remember that:

1. Life insurance is usually the major source of liquidity to beneficiaries.
2. Life insurance proceeds, in most states, are exempt from the claims of the deceased's creditors.
3. Life insurance proceeds are usually not subject to probate, by either probate expenses or probate delays.

However, many life insurance policies also contain investment features which can be used to provide additional income for you and your family. You probably won't want to buy life insurance primarily for its investment value—other forms of investments are generally more lucrative—but the investment benefits can be a significant secondary reason for buying insurance, as well as a factor in choosing among the available policies. So it pays to understand the different types of life insurance and their varying values as investments.

Let's consider the most popular forms of life insurance today, with special attention to their investment potential: (1) term insurance, (2) straight life insurance, (3) universal life insurance, and (4) single-premium whole life insurance.

How Does Term Insurance Work?

Term life insurance offers the greatest amount of financial protection at the lowest cost in premiums. This is because when you buy term insurance, you buy the possible death benefit only; there is no savings or investment of a specified sum if you die during the life of the policy (the "term" from which this type of insurance gets its name). Term policies are usually issued for a specific period of years, after which the insurance coverage can be renewed but only at a higher premium rate.

Two variations on the term insurance policy are the *decreasing term* policy, in which the premiums remain the same but the amount of the death benefit decreases as you get older, and the *level term* policy, in which the amount of the death benefit remains the same but the size of the premium increases over time.

Term insurance is popular in instances where the need for life insurance protection is temporary or where other, more costly forms of insurance are unaffordable. For example, term insurance may be an ideal choice for a young family with children, where insurance protection is vital but the family income may still be modest. As the family grows older and the parents' careers take wing, the family income will probably increase, and other types of policies may become more attractive. But remember this: Although the premiums of term will eventually become more expensive than the cash-value policies mentioned in the next few pages, term has the advantage of being far less costly at the time in people's lives when large amounts of coverage are most needed.

How Does Straight Life Insurance Work?

Also known as *whole life insurance,* a straight life policy offers a specified death benefit (the face value of the policy) in exchange for an unchanging premium payment. The size of the premium depends mainly on your age at the time you purchase the policy; the younger you are, the lower your annual premium will be. At the time of your death, the face value of the policy will be paid to your beneficiary.

Unlike term insurance, straight life insurance includes an investment feature. Part of your premium payment is placed in a savings fund and invested by the insurance company. As the years pass, the amount of money in this fund will grow both from your contributions and from the company's investment earnings. This growing sum is known as the policy's *cash surrender value.* It is quite small at first but, after a number of years, can become a substantial amount of money. The cash surrender value of your policy can benefit you in two ways. First, if you terminate the policy, you can receive the cash surrender value as a lump sum (unlike term insurance, where you walk away with nothing). Second, while the policy is in force, you can borrow against the cash surrender value at a favorable interest rate, even if you may not qualify for other types of loans. This provision can be useful, for example, when college tuition bills come due.

The investment value of straight life insurance gives it an advantage over term insurance. However, it is considerably more costly. The amount of savings you'll accumulate through your insurance policy is probably smaller than the amount you could save through other investment plans. And, of course, in order for your beneficiary to receive the death benefit, you must continue to pay premiums until you die. This can be a financial strain, especially for older people whose earnings have fallen after retirement. So consider the pros and cons carefully before opting for a straight life policy.

How Does Universal Life Insurance Work?

Because of much criticism about insurance companies' low returns on whole life policies, the concept of *universal life insurance* was born. Unlike deferred annuities, the universal life policy is bought mainly for its insurance feature. It was first introduced in 1979 as a type of life insurance which combines insurance protection (in the form of term insurance coverage) with a savings plan that builds tax-deferred income at highly competitive rates. This income becomes taxable only when the policy lapses or is surrendered. The holder of a universal life policy chooses the amount of life insurance protection he or she wants, and part of the premium goes to cover that protection. The rest of the premium payment is invested by the insurance company in various high-yielding investments. Watch out for these yields though. Although high, they are usually "gross" rates, meaning that administrative and other costs have not been considered in the computation. The insurance company's investment managers usually decide on the investment policy, so your growth or yield is determined by their decisions. If the managers make a series of bad investment decisions, the cash value of your policy will decline. This doesn't happen with straight life insurance, where cash values are projected using a fixed interest rate, so that you know in advance just what your policy's cash surrender value will be at any time.

Another important feature to consider is that this type of policy is very flexible. At any time, the amount of insurance coverage can be increased or decreased, the size of the premiums can be adjusted, and the accumulated cash value can be withdrawn by means of an automatic policy loan.

An interesting option that is offered with some universal life policies, known as a *vanishing premium,* allows you to discontinue your payments after a certain period of time. Assume you are 40 years old. You will pay a larger premium for a fixed number of years (I'll use 25 years as an example). After the twenty-fifth year the earnings on the premiums will have accumulated and the premiums will be paid from the earnings. So, by the time you are ready for retirement, you no longer have to worry about paying life insurance premiums. Remember that the death benefit does not decline when you stop paying premiums.

And one last point. If the earnings on the universal life policy are more than what the company had projected, you may find that the death benefit actually increases. The reason is that by tax law, the cash value of the policy cannot be allowed to come too close to the policy's death benefit. If this should occur, the death benefit must be increased or the policy would lose its tax-favored status.

Therefore, when shopping for universal life insurance, it's very important to compare the investment policies of different insurance companies. Some are more successful than others. Also find out about the fees charged by the companies you're considering. Some charge heavy sales commissions, which may run as high as 50 percent of your first year's premium; others charge large surrender fees (known as *back-end loads*) in the event you decide to cancel your policy. Ask before you buy.

How Does Single-Premium Whole Life Work?

Single-premium whole life (SPWL) is much like universal life in that it offers a tax-free buildup of cash coupled with life insurance. Its main attraction is not the insurance coverage as in universal life, but in its returns. The SPWL is designed so that it carries just enough insurance to qualify for tax-free status, with most of the premium going for earnings instead of high insurance protection.

How Does the Policy Act as an Investment?

This type of life insurance uses a market-sensitive interest rate or a choice of mutual funds. Although the policy pays a death benefit, its big attraction is what is does for you while you are still alive. With this policy you pay one lump-sum amount (usually $5000 to $50,000) and receive insurance and tax-free deferred savings.

There are two types of single-premium whole life policies. With a *fixed* whole life, the policy usually pays a set return and is adjusted annually with a guaranteed floor. The other type (*variable*) puts premiums into stocks, bonds, mutual funds, etc., with its return unpredictable, as its yield is based on the performance of the instruments in which it has been invested.

The key item is that your earnings accumulate tax-deferred. Upon the policyholder's death, the beneficiaries receive the face value of the policy tax-free. But the important item is not death but life. You can borrow against the cash value at little or no cost—tax-free. But watch out that you don't dip too deeply into the policy, as your insurance coverage could lapse, triggering a tax bill on all the earnings.

The best method of comparing which type of policy to buy is to ask each insurer for the total cost per $1000 of coverage. But beware; there are pitfalls. The cost can be high. In the fixed whole life, the insurance company pays you at least one percentage point less than what it is making on your money, and in variable whole life, the insurance company keeps all management fees.

What Are the Characteristics of the SPWL?

1. There is a minimum $5000 contribution.

2. Your earnings accumulate tax-free.

3. You can borrow against earnings or principal at low rates with *no tax* consequences.

4. Proceeds of the policy at your death go to your beneficiaries.

5. It can be a savings plan for college. You can pay a fixed amount, let the interest accrue tax-deferred until the child reaches college age, and then borrow the cost of tuition (tax-free) from the policy. You have the added benefit of being covered by life insurance should a parent die before the child enters college.

What Should You Remember about Choosing a Policy?

On the basis of the brief descriptions in this chapter, if you consider your objectives, you will now be able to choose the best type of policy for you. Term insurance is your choice if your needs require large amounts of insurance and you cannot afford cash-value policies. Consider straight life, universal, or SPWL only if you can afford the higher premiums. Remember that you should not forsake important coverage for investment yield. Also, the tax-deferred features of the investment-type policies are of most benefit to people in high tax brackets. If you are not in a high tax bracket, you may be better off in a taxable investment paying a higher rate even though the interest is subject to tax. And on the topic of life insurance, as the insurance agent said, "Don't let me push you into making a hasty decision. Sleep on it tonight. If you should wake up tomorrow, let me know what you've decided."

10

Money Market Accounts—The Parking Lot

The idea is to make a little money first and then to make a little money last.

As far as I am concerned, the money market is nothing more than a parking lot, a temporary area for buying and selling high-yield, short-term instruments of credit. In the money market, securities such as Treasury bills, certificates of deposit, and short-term commercial loans are bought and sold. Since these securities carry high interest rates, they make money grow quickly. But they normally require extremely large investments (Treasury bills, $10,000; jumbo CDs and commercial paper, $100,000) that only wealthy individuals or large institutions could previously afford. That's where the money market funds came in. First made available in 1974, money market funds offered the small investor a chance to take advantage of the interest rates prevailing in the money markets by pooling many people's money.

How Does a Money Market Account Work?

Money market funds operate by combining many small investors' funds to accumulate the kind of money needed to buy the costly money market instruments just mentioned (jumbo CDs, T-bills, etc.). Since the instruments purchased by the fund have different maturities, the fund earns interest on a daily basis. Each investor receives his or her share of the interest by means of a regular statement, usually issued monthly. The amount earned on an investment varies continually as the prevalent interest rates in the money market rise and fall.

Money market funds are managed by investment firms and brokerage houses that charge a management fee which is deducted from the fund's earnings. Usually no redemption charges are imposed on the fund. Most firms transact business by mail, so a money market fund headquartered in Illinois, for example, may have shareholders in any of the 50 states. A minimum deposit is required to open a money market account; $1000 is typical. You can add to your investment at any time, and your funds are completely liquid—you can make withdrawals whenever you wish. Many money market funds allow you to withdraw your money simply by writing a check, although there is usually a limit on the number of checks that you are permitted to write (minimum from $100 to $500 per check). Thus you may want to consider using a money market fund in place of a conventional checking account.

What Types of Money Market Funds Are Offered?

Money market funds can be broken into three categories, based upon the type of instruments in which the funds invest.

1. *General money market funds:* These invest primarily in non-governmental securities, such as bank certificates of deposit, commercial loans, and banker's acceptances. Of the three types of funds, general money market funds usually pay the highest interest rates.

2. *Government-only money market funds:* These invest only in securities issued by the U.S. government or by a federal

agency. These funds boast a somewhat higher degree of safety than the general money market funds, but they pay a little less.

3. *Tax-free money market funds:* These purchase only short-term, tax-exempt municipal bonds and are especially suitable for investors in high tax brackets. Although this type of money market fund is exempt from federal tax, some funds will still be subject to state and local income taxes since most states do not exempt taxes on municipals issued out of state. The exceptions are Alaska, Florida, Indiana, Nebraska, New Mexico, South Dakota, Utah, Vermont, Washington, Wyoming, and the District of Columbia. If you reside in a state with a high income tax, search out those municipal money market funds that purchase investments only within your state of residence. For example, a fund may obtain only Massachusetts securities so that all of the income earned will be "triple-tax-free" to Massachusetts investors. However, Illinois, Iowa, Kansas, Oklahoma, and Wisconsin will impose a tax on municipal bonds issued within their state. And another important point about this type of tax-free fund: If you are subject to the AMT (alternative minimum tax), make certain you examine the portfolio of the tax-free fund to be sure that it does not contain those types of bonds whose interest has to be included in the minimum tax computation. This would include certain private-purpose (industrial development, student loans, housing) tax-exempt bonds issued after August 1986.

Because of the liquidity of your investment in a money market fund, it is an ideal way to invest idle cash that might otherwise find its way into a low-paying passbook savings account. For example, placing the proceeds from the sale of securities into a money market fund until you've decided upon your next investment venture is a good way of earning continuous high interest on your money. Also, many money market funds are part of a larger group of other types of funds (known as a *family of funds*) that permit you to move your money from one investment to another as financial conditions change. The most prominent funds are listed daily in the financial sections of newspapers. These listings show the average maturity (the shorter the time, the faster the fund reacts to changes in interest rates) and the average yield for the previous 7 days. If you are interested in obtaining a list of money funds and their toll-free numbers, you can write to the Investment Company Institute, 1600 N Street, N.W., Washington, DC 20036.

How Do Money Markets Issued by Banks Work?

Banks have now entered the money market field with their version of the money market fund, the *money market deposit account* (MMDA). The MMDA was first authorized by Congress in 1982 in order to stem the $200 billion tide of withdrawals the banks claimed were lured away by the money market funds. Yet you do not hear much about them because they are not adequately advertised. You see, the banks would rather you purchase their CDs because with a CD they will have your money for a longer period of time.

The MMDA is similar in many ways to the money market fund. It too is based on the pooling concept, allowing small investors to earn interest rates otherwise reserved for large institutional investors or wealthy individuals. Like a money market fund, an MMDA requires a minimum initial deposit as well as a minimum balance. However, as of 1986 federal regulations no longer required a minimum MMDA balance; banks became free to enforce a minimum balance rule at their own discretion, so don't blame the government if your bank requires a high minimum balance.

Finally, as with a money market fund, an MMDA is a good way to invest cash for a short period.

What Are the Major Differences between the Money Market Fund and the MMDA?

When you invest in a money market fund, you become a shareholder in the fund. You and the other shareholders receive all the income earned by the fund's investments, less a small management fee (usually about ½ percent annually). When you invest in an MMDA, on the other hand, you are not a shareholder but simply a depositor. Investors in MMDAs do not necessarily receive all the interest generated by investments, but receive whatever interest rate the bank chooses to pay. Furthermore, the bank is free to invest your money any way it sees fit, even in investments that have little or nothing to do with the money market. Therefore, you have no guarantee that the interest rate you receive will truly reflect the money market rate.

Note, too, the difference in the way the money market funds and the MMDAs usually advertise the interest rates they pay. Money market funds normally advertise the current simple interest rate being earned by the fund. This yield, which is not guaranteed, can change daily as conditions in the money markets change. By contrast, banks often promote MMDAs by advertising the effective yield rate, which is usually a fraction of a point higher than the simple interest rate because of compounding. However, the effective yield rate can be misleading, as it assumes that the bank will be giving compound interest on an unchanging interest rate for a full year. Since this is highly unlikely to occur, you should take with a grain of salt the high effective yields claimed by banks.

Therefore, these lower-yielding instruments will lag behind those with shorter maturities and thus could cause a loss in the fund's market value. The average maturity for investments held by general money market funds is about 35 days; for the tax-free funds, about 65 days.

There are other differences between money market funds and MMDAs to consider:

1. With an MMDA, you have a person-to-person relationship with a bank officer whom you know, rather than the kind of anonymous, through-the-mail relationship usually offered by the money market funds. For some investors, dealing with a personal banker is psychologically important.

2. The money market fund may be preferable if you plan on making frequent withdrawals from your account. You are usually permitted unlimited withdrawals by check from the fund. With an MMDA, there is normally a limit of three checks per month. However, in most banks you can make deposits or withdrawals 24 hours a day by means of the bank's automated teller machines (ATMs), which you cannot do with the money market fund.

3. With an MMDA, you may lose up to a month's interest if you close out your account during that period. With a money market fund, this cannot happen because of daily payments of interest.

Are Both the Money Market Fund and the MMDA Safe Investments?

As with any form of investment, safety is a factor to consider. Your investment in an MMDA offered by a bank or a savings and loan institution is insured by the federal government according to the rules governing the maximum of $100,000. If safety is of overriding importance to you, choose an MMDA over a money market fund. However, you should realize that the money market funds have an excellent safety track record. This is because they invest only in short-term instruments issued by such secure institutions as government agencies, large corporations, and major banks. An investor's rule of thumb is that the shorter the maturity of an investment, the lower the risk. Why is this? If interest rates should rapidly rise, funds holding long-term maturities would find it more difficult to liquidate their low-yielding holdings. Further-more, the Securities and Exchange Commission (SEC) regulates money market funds very strictly.

Therefore, the concept of the money market is simple.

1. The principal you invest is safe.

2. You can withdraw your money at any time with no penalty.

3. You'll earn interest rates that reflect up-to-date market conditions.

This combination of benefits makes money market investing one of today's most popular investment options. And on the topic of investing, money never changes, only pockets.

11

Mortgages—
The Finances of
Home Ownership

*Love your neighbor—but don't pull down the
fences.*

For most people, buying a home entails taking out a mortgage to help meet the cost of purchase. You are normally required to pay a percentage of the purchase price in cash; this is called the *down payment*. The remainder of the purchase price is covered by the mortgage, with your title to the house used as security for the unpaid balance on your mortgage. This means that if you are unable to repay your mortgage, the lender has the right to foreclose, that is, to take possession of the property. Most mortgage loans are made by banks and savings and loan associations, though other institutions and individuals may sometimes offer mortgages.

What Must You Know about a Mortgage?

There are four terms that are essential in understanding mortgages.

1. *Origination fee:* This is a one-time charge that the lender will add as a cost of the mortgage.

2. *Simple interest rate:* This is the quoted rate of the loan. If a mortgage is negotiated for 25 years at 11 percent with a 3 point origination fee, the simple interest is still 11 percent.

3. *Effective interest rate:* This is different from the simple rate in that it is the actual cost of borrowing after considering origination fees. In the preceding example the effective rate would be 11.42 percent.

4. *PITI:* This stands for the total monthly payment of *principal, interest, taxes, and insurance* that is so important to know when a family budgets for the purchase of a home.

What Types of Mortgages Are Offered?

Many mortgages provide for repayment over a 10- to 30-year period in equal monthly payment amounts based on a fixed rate of interest. Each payment includes both repayment of principal and payment of interest, with early payments representing interest and later payments representing mainly principal. This is known as the fixed-rate mortgage payment. However, the volatile economic climate of the late 1970s—in particular, soaring interest rates—led to the increased use of another type of mortgage, the *adjustable-rate mortgage* (ARM). This type of mortgage is usually a long-term loan, providing for repayment in 20 or 30 years. It differs from the traditional fixed-rate mortgage in that the interest rate on the loan changes at stated intervals. Thus, as interest rates rise, the amount you must pay the bank each month rises too; as interest rates fall, so do your monthly payments.

How Does the ARM Work?

The amount you must pay each month on an adjustable-rate mortgage loan depends on three factors:

1. *Interval:* The period of time between adjustments of the interest rate. Typical intervals are 6 months and 1 year.

2. *Index:* A guideline used in determining the current interest rate on the mortgage. The index will be clearly defined at the time the mortgage is made. Any of a number of widely accepted financial guidelines may be used as an index; one typical index is the current interest rate on 6-month U.S. Treasury bills. As the index goes up or down, so does the interest rate on your mortgage, and along with it your monthly payment.

3. *Cap:* A predetermined figure limiting the movement of the interest rate on your mortgage in any single interval. If an adjustable-rate mortgage includes a cap, and not all do, the interest rate may not change by an amount greater than the cap, even though the variation in the index would normally call for a greater change.

As you can see, an adjustable-rate mortgage has one major disadvantage for the borrower: It's impossible to know beforehand how large your monthly payments will be in the future. Thus much of the security of the traditional fixed-rate mortgage is forfeited. In many cases, an adjustable-rate mortgage is offered at a lower initial interest rate than a comparable fixed-rate mortgage, but you won't know how long this advantage will last. Therefore, it is better for most home buyers to obtain (for their peace of mind) the fixed-rate mortgage—if one is available.

How Does Refinancing a Mortgage Work in Today's Market?

Where possible, it may be advantageous for you to switch mortgage methods by refinancing if interest rates go down. But it is not always true that a lower interest rate alone means that refinancing is the way to go. For example, it could take many years to recoup the cost of the up-front fees, which

could include lawyer's fees, title search and insurance, recording taxes, and, possibly, bank origination fees. Table 11.1
shows the cost of refinancing and is based on a trade-in of a
present 30-year, $100,000 mortgage for a new, fixed-rate
mortgage at 9.5 percent costing $840 a month. It also takes
into consideration total closing costs of $3000 with no prepay-
ment penalty clause.

TABLE 11.1.	COST OF REFINANCING		
Original mortgage rate, %	Current monthly payment	Monthly savings at 9.5 percent	Time to recoup costs, months
10.0	$ 878	$ 38	82
10.5	914	74	41
11.0	951	111	27
11.5	990	150	20
12.0	1028	188	16
12.5	1067	227	13
13.0	1106	266	11
13.5	1145	305	10

In comparing figures in the table, you must also consider
the tax consequences before any refinancing decision can
take place. Remember, by reducing your mortgage payment
(which includes tax-deductible interest), you reduce the only
tax deduction for interest which is left for the middle-income
investor. This then raises your taxable income. So think carefully and weigh all the factors necessary to make an intelligent choice. As a rule of thumb, do not refinance your existing mortgage unless you can benefit by at least 2 percentage
points off the old mortgage rate.

I believe that the fixed-rate mortgage payment is the most
desirable kind, but it may be difficult to obtain in some areas,

TABLE 11.2. MONTHLY MORTGAGE PAYMENTS FOR EACH $1000 OWED

Interest rate, %	Years				
	10	15	20	25	30
9.5	$12.94	$10.45	$ 9.33	$ 8.74	$ 8.41
10.0	13.22	10.75	9.66	9.09	8.78
10.5	13.50	11.06	9.99	9.45	9.14
11.0	13.78	11.37	10.33	9.81	9.51
11.5	14.06	11.69	10.67	10.17	9.90
12.0	14.35	12.01	11.02	10.54	10.28
12.5	14.64	12.33	11.37	10.91	10.67
13.0	14.94	12.66	11.72	11.28	11.06
13.5	15.23	12.99	12.08	11.66	11.45

especially on a long-term basis. Table 11.2 shows the monthly mortgage payments under a fixed-rate mortgage. For example, a $50,000 mortgage at 11% for 20 years would be calculated as $10.33 (look under 11 percent and across to 20 years) × 50 = $516.50 per monthly payment. If the mortgage loan were $75,000, you would multiply $10.33 by 75 to get $774.75.

What Are the Tax Considerations in Mortgage Financing?

No matter which type or mortgage you obtain, you'll receive significant tax benefits during the repayment period. These benefits arise from the fact that interest payments on the original purchase of a home, up to $1 million, are deductible from your taxable income for federal income tax purposes. For most homeowners, that's a substantial amount.

If you're currently shopping for a home (and a mortgage),

you should be aware of two other factors which will affect the cost of home buying: closing costs and points.

Closing costs are one-time expenses that include the cost of a title search, title insurance, surveying fees, attorneys' fees, mortgage recording tax, and many other smaller fees that can total as much as 5 percent of the value of the home you're buying. Before purchase, you should receive from the lending institution a good-faith estimate of what your closing costs will be.

Points are one-time lump-sum charges levied by the bank at the time you buy your home. A point is 1 percent of the total amount of the loan; the bank may charge from 2 to 4 points. For example, if you take out a $60,000 mortgage from a bank which charges 4 points for the loan, you will have to pay the bank a $2400 fee at the time of purchase. To receive the most for your money, you should estimate how long you intend to own the home. Then decide, on the basis of the figures in Table 11.3, the best combination of interest rate and points. Because points are an up-front fee, whether you sell your

TABLE 11.3. COST OF MORTGAGE INCLUDING POINTS		
	Rate	
Points	10%	11%
Paid in 30 Years		
1	10.12%	11.13%
2	10.24%	11.26%
3	10.37%	11.39%
Paid in 15 Years		
1	10.14%	11.14%
2	10.28%	11.29%
3	10.42%	11.44%

house and pay off the loan after only 15 years or 30 years, remember that the longer you hold the loan, the smaller the impact the points will have on the effective rate of the mortgage.

If the payment of points is properly executed, it is usually deductible in the year you take out the mortgage. How can you make certain whether you will get the tax deduction? The best method is to ask the lender whether the points are considered a prepayment of interest or a service fee. Prepayment of interest is deductible, while a service fee is not.

If the bank certified that the points represent a prepayment of interest, make doubly sure of your deduction by paying the points with a separate check. Don't allow the bank to deduct the points from the mortgage. Suppose, for instance, you borrow $60,000 and owe 4 points. Don't accept a check from the bank for $57,600 ($60,000 less the $2400 payment of points). Instead, ask for payment of the full mortgage amount, and then hand over your own check for $2400. Note that this does not apply to the refinancing of a home. The tax law states that you can deduct points only on a mortgage incurred "in connection with" the purchase of your principal residence. This means that the "all at once" deduction is limited to the mortgage you first take out when you buy your home and not to its refinancing, as with a home equity loan; with refinancing, you must amortize (spread out) the point cost over the life of the loan.

What Is a Home Equity Loan?

Up to this point, we've been concentrating on the most common type of mortgage loan—the "first mortgage"—normally taken out to make home purchase possible. However, many homeowners who already have mortgages are now taking advantage of the equity they have built up in their homes by borrowing against that equity. These loans are called *home equity loans* and are a convenient source of needed cash. Many banks will lend up to 80 percent of the equity of your home—that is, the value of your home less the unpaid balance of your mortgage—without requiring lengthy loan applications or long waits for approval. After you take out a home equity loan, you will have to make two monthly loan repayments (one for the original mortgage and one for the second mortgage) to retain your ownership of a single piece of property.

Like first mortgages, home equity loans have varying terms. When a fixed interest rate is charged, the term is usually 15 years or less; when the interest rate is variable, the term may be up to 20 years or in some cases even longer. The payback period on this second mortgage is usually shorter than on the first mortgage. In addition, you may be charged one or more extra points for a home equity loan, but today many banks are waiving this extra cost. Also, although the points are deductible for refinancing on home equity loans, as stated before, they cannot be deducted all at once but must be gradually written off over the years that you remain in the house. On the original purchase of a home, however, you can deduct the cost of the points at one time.

Immediately after the 1986 Tax Reform Act, the public found that they had lost most of their interest deductions on personal debt. But by taking out a home equity loan, they were still able to deduct the interest charges regardless of the purpose the funds were used for. The laws have changed slightly, but within the limits of sensible debt management it is still advantageous to secure a home equity loan when you need money. And this has become the loan's greatest advantage. This type of borrowing is an ideal method for financing a child's education: It is often less expensive than a normal personal loan, the interest you are charged is tax-deductible, and the payback period can be spread over 20 years. Or you may use the funds for needed medical expenses or for just "you" and that dream "retreat" that you were never able to afford. In today's economy, financing for vacation homes is not always readily available, and when it is, it is usually encumbered with stringent restrictions. Now, through home equity loans, these impossible dreams can become a reality.

And on the topic of mortgages, it is amazing that yesterday's nest egg can't buy today's birdhouse.

12
Municipal Bonds— The Tax-Free Choice

You work hard all your life to reach a high
tax bracket and then the government goes
and lowers it on you.

With major changes to, or even the total loss of, our personal deductions (sales tax, medical expenses, consumer interest, casualty losses, etc.) because of the Tax Reform Act, and with the increases in the social security tax base, the desire for untaxed income (such as that available from the municipal bond) has become stronger than ever. Since these tax-exempt bonds yield about 85 percent of comparable taxable issues, the investor in the 28 to 31 percent tax bracket has a chance to lock in excellent returns.

How Do Municipal Bonds Work?

Today, few local or state governments have on hand the vast sums of money needed to build schools, roads, water and sewer facilities, and other public works. Some towns, cities, and counties are finding it difficult even to meet their daily operating expenses. But these social needs won't just disappear. In order to meet these expenses, communities borrow money from citizens and institutions by issuing debt obligations known as *municipal bonds* (*munis*). There are over 40,000 different government units and agencies currently issuing municipal bonds. They include states, cities, towns, counties, and such agencies as highway departments and housing authorities. The Tax Reform Act imposed restrictions (loss of tax-exempt status and a new, toughened alternative tax) on some newly issued municipal bonds that finance private projects (such as convention centers or sports stadiums) in excess of certain dollar amounts. However, bonds issued before September 1986 generally will retain their tax-free status regardless of the date on which they were acquired. Also, the average investor who purchases municipal bonds for public use (water and sewer districts, highways, etc.) will not be affected by tax reform, and the income generated from these public activity bonds will remain tax-free.

What Types of Municipal Bonds Are Available?

Among the varieties of more popular municipal bonds commonly available are the following:

1. *General obligation (GO) bonds:* These are backed by the full faith and credit of the issuing agency. Interest payments on GO bonds are supported by the taxing authority of the state or city government and are generally considered the safest form of municipal bonds.

2. *Revenue bonds:* These are usually issued by a government agency or commission that has been charged with operating a self-supporting project such as a highway or bridge. The money raised through the sale of revenue bonds goes to finance the project, and the income realized from the completed project (tolls, for example) is used to pay the interest and principal on the bonds. However, if the project earns insufficient income, bondholders may be left holding the bag; the taxpayers of the community are not responsible. Therefore, your risk is greater in buying revenue bonds, but your yield is a bit higher.

What Are the Advantages and Disadvantages of Municipal Bonds?

The advantages of municipal bonds are as follows.

1. *Tax exemption:* For the investor, the most important advantage of municipal bonds is the fact that they earn income which is tax-free at the federal level. If you live in a state in which the bonds are issued, the bonds are usually free from state and local income taxes as well.

2. *Safety:* Municipal bonds have historically been a very safe form of investment, as states and cities, with their power of taxation, have normally been able to fully meet their debt obligations.

3. *High collateral value:* It's usually possible to borrow up to 90 percent of the market value of your municipal bonds from such lenders as banks and brokerage houses, since municipal bonds are free of certain restrictions imposed by the Federal Reserve Board on the use of other bonds as collateral.

4. *Diversity:* Thousands of different municipal bonds are available to meet the requirements of individual investors.

5. *Marketability:* A large nationwide market for municipal bonds exists, making them easy to sell when necessary. However, you should never buy municipal bonds for speculation. Purchase them for the tax-free income they produce and only in anticipation of what you can get *from* them, not *for* them.

Attractive as these features may be, municipal bonds are not for everyone.

1. *Investment:* Fairly sizable investment is needed, with a minimum investment of $5000 usually required.

2. *Yield:* Tax-exempt municipal bonds usually carry a lower rate of interest than taxable bonds. If the tax rate you pay is fairly high, your tax savings will more than make up for

the lower return; but those near the bottom of the tax rate tables may be better off with another investment.

3. *Social security:* If you are collecting social security benefits, there may be a problem because, although the interest you receive from these bonds is not taxable for federal purposes, you may have to pay tax on up to half your social security benefits (see pages 186 to 188).

Are Municipals Your Best Investment?

To determine whether or not you should invest in municipal bonds, you must figure out the taxable rate of return equivalent to that paid by tax-exempt municipals. For example, suppose you are in an income tax bracket of 28 percent, and you are offered a tax-exempt municipal bond paying 7 percent interest. To find the equivalent taxable rate of return: (1) take the difference between your tax rate and 100 percent, and (2) divide this into the interest rate paid by the tax-exempt bond. Since your tax rate is 28 percent, the difference between this and 100 percent is 72 percent. Divide 72 into 7 and you obtain a result of 9.7 percent. Thus, a tax-exempt interest rate of 7 percent is equivalent to a taxable interest rate of 9.7 percent for someone in the 28 percent tax bracket.

The formula below will help you determine the equivalent taxable yield (ETY):

$$ETY = \frac{\text{yield on muni}}{1.00 - \text{tax bracket}}$$

$$= \frac{7\%}{1.00 - 0.28} \quad \text{or} \quad \frac{7\%}{0.72} = 9.7\%$$

Table 12.1 shows several typical tax-exempt interest rates along with the equivalent taxable yield for investors in various tax brackets. For example, this table shows that for an investor in the 28 percent tax bracket, a 7 percent tax-exempt yield is equivalent to a 9.7 percent taxable yield and a 10.1 percent yield if you consider the surcharge.

TABLE 12.1. EQUIVALENT TAXABLE YIELD			
Tax-exempt bond rate, %	Income tax rate		
	15%	28%	31%*
6	7.0%	8.3%	8.7%
7	8.2%	9.7%	10.1%
7.5	8.8%	10.4%	10.9%
8	9.4%	11.1%	11.5%

*Reflects surcharge for 1991.

The equivalent taxable yield of 9.7 percent means that you would need to find a taxable instrument paying almost 10 percent to equal your 7 percent tax-exempt bond. By using this table, you will be able to determine the type of taxable return you would have to receive to exceed the tax-exempt return from your muni. Also, bear in mind that state tax is not considered in this example, so your yield is actually higher than 9.7 percent.

In order to find the taxable equivalent yield of a state-exempt municipal, multiply the state yield by the taxable equivalent factor of your federal income tax bracket (28 percent or additional surcharge) (see Table 12.2). This procedure will show what a taxable bond would have to pay to equal the return of the municipal bond. Kidder, Peabody, which compiled these multipliers (April 1990), figured into them the effects of federal and state income taxes, including any peculiarities of state law. Top marginal state tax rates are used, but there is a factor that reduces the multiplier because deductions from federal returns and other tax treatments (where appropriate) are considered. To find the taxable equivalent yield of a state-exempt municipal, multiply the state yield by the taxable equivalent factor shown for the tax bracket of the state in which the investor lives. For example, in Massachusetts, the taxable equivalent of 7.00 percent for

TABLE 12.2. A PROFILE OF STATE TAXES: TAXABLE EQUIVALENT "FACTORS"*

State	Federal tax rate 28%	State	Federal tax rate 28%
Alabama	1.442	Montana	1.519
Alaska†	1.389	Nebraska	1.476
Arizona	1.476	Nevada†	1.389
Arkansas	1.493	New Hampshire	1.462
California	1.531	New Jersey	1.493
Colorado	1.458	New Mexico	1.507
Connecticut	1.615	N.Y. State	1.499
Delaware	1.505	NYC/NYS	1.557
D.C.	1.535	North Carolina	1.493
Florida	‡	North Dakota	1.455
Georgia	1.472	Ohio	1.492
Hawaii	1.528	Oklahoma	1.478
Idaho	1.513	Oregon	1.526
Illinois	1.432	Pennsylvania	1.419
Indiana	1.438	Rhode Island	1.478
Iowa	1.500	South Carolina	1.493
Kansas	1.485	South Dakota†	1.389
Kentucky	1.453	Tennessee	1.478
Louisiana	1.453	Texas	1.389
Maine	1.518	Utah	1.482
Maryland	1.502	Vermont	1.486
Massachusetts	1.543	Virginia	1.474
Michigan	1.511	West Virginia	1.485
Minnesota	1.510	Washington†	1.389
Mississippi	1.458	Wisconsin	1.492
Missouri	1.485	Wyoming†	1.389

*Copyright © 1990 by Kidder, Peabody & Co. Incorporated. Reproduced by permission.

†These states currently do not impose a state income tax.

‡While Florida has no income tax, there is a 1 mill per $1 market value ($1 per $1000) intangible personal property tax on holding of securities. Municipals issued within Florida are exempt.

an investor in the 28 percent federal tax bracket is 1.5443 ×
7.00%, or 10.80%. For the surcharge bracket, it would be
1.658 × 7.00%, or 11.61%. Note that although interest from
many municipal bonds is taxed in Colorado, Illinois, Iowa,
Kansas, Oklahoma, and Wisconsin, the figures presented in
Table 12.2 assume you own the bonds exempt from the state
income tax.

Are Municipals a Risky Investment?

As with any investment, risk is a factor to consider in purchasing municipal bonds. Like corporate bonds, municipal bonds
are rated by two major independent rating services, Moody's
and Standard & Poor's. The AAA rating is the highest. In general, the lower the rating, the higher the yield. However, I
don't recommend that you purchase bonds with low ratings,
as the slightly higher interest rate you may be offered on the
lower-rated bond isn't worth the sacrifice in safety. Also, when
financial times are uncertain, investors will look for quality
bonds even though they produce a lower yield.

One way to virtually eliminate the risk in buying municipal
bonds is to buy bonds that carry a third-party guarantee offered by companies such as the Municipal Bond Insurance
Association (MBIA), the Financial Guaranty Insurance Company (FGIC), Capital Guaranty (CG), or the American Municipal Bond Assurance Corporation (AMBAC). MBIA,
AMBAC, and FGIC are rated AAA by both Standard & Poor's
and Moody's. CG, which is rated only by Standard & Poor's,
also has a AAA rating. If the issuing agency should fail, the insurer will continue to make timely payments of interest and
principal as agreed upon at the time of purchase. In addition,
the insurance will add to the liquidity of the investment, since
potential buyers appreciate the greater safety of the insured
bonds.

Here's how it works. When a municipality issues muni
bonds, the city's or state's credit is on the line. If the bonds
are low-rated, the municipality must pay higher than normal

interest on the issued bonds. To save money, it may purchase insurance which guarantees that all payments of principal and interest will be paid in time. For example, a city offering a bond with a BBB rating could pay a one-time premium (about 1 percent) and receive a major boost in its issue to AA or even AAA. It thus may appear that the insurance is free to the investor, but that is not true. Since the insurance raises the quality of the bond's credit, the yield on the bond issued will be lower. And one more point. The cost-yield difference between an insured and an uninsured bond is so narrow that today the insurance has become a "good buy."

Can Municipal Bonds Be Called Back?

Callability is a significant factor affecting the value of municipal bonds. Bonds that offer interest rates that are higher than what is presently being offered are most likely to be called in because the issuer will want to redeem these costly older bonds and replace them with new ones paying lower yields. It may be good for the municipality issuing them, but it is certainly bad for the bondholder who loses the higher yield. When a bond is callable, it may be redeemed by the issuing agency prior to the maturity date, usually within 5 to 10 years after issue, and usually at a premium over the face value of the bond. Of course, this places a lid on potential profits, which may be a significant loss to you if interest rates decline greatly after the bond is issued. Even the premium paid on redemption—typically about 2 percent—is usually less than the market value of the bond. So, if possible, try to buy bonds that are noncallable.

Are There Strategies in Purchasing Municipal Bonds?

One method of diversifying a bond portfolio is a technique known as *laddering*. What is done is that you purchase bonds that mature in different years. Therefore, if rates have risen when a bond matures, you will be able to reinvest the proceeds into an instrument paying the new high yield. Conversely, if interest rates should fall, a portion of your holdings will still earn interest at the higher (earlier) rates.

Also, look into *pre-refunded premium bonds*. These bonds are issued by states and municipalities in order to reduce the high double-digit interest costs of bonds issued by them during the early 1980s. What happens is that the issuer will sell, at a lower rate, a second series of bonds maturing on the date when the old bonds can be called in early. The proceeds of the second series are invested in Treasuries, and this gives safety to the old issues.

How Do You Find the Best Bond Value?

Get quotes from several brokers before buying bonds. Prices on previously issued bonds vary greatly from dealer to dealer, as each sets his or her own profit margin individually. The difference between what the broker pays for the bond (known as the *bid price*) and its selling price (known as the *asking price*) is the *spread*. Brokers do not charge commissions on bond trades but make their money on this difference (quoted in basis points which are hundredths of a percentage point). Each point of this spread takes off $\frac{1}{100}$ of 1 percent from your yield and costs you 0.01 percent. Remember, the longer the maturity and the smaller the trade, the wider the spread. Before buying, ask your broker what he or she would pay to buy the bond back on the following day. This question exposes any hidden charges such as fees and markups. The matter is further complicated by the fact that municipal bonds are not listed on any exchange, making it that much harder to gauge prices. This caveat doesn't apply to new issues; the issuer pays the dealer's markup on those, so that you'll get the best price no matter where you buy. Therefore, seek out all information before purchasing. And on the topic of information, the tree of knowledge is watered by tears of experience.

13

Municipal Trusts and Funds— Tax-Free Alternatives

It may be true that there are two sides to every alternative, but it is also true that there are two sides to a sheet of flypaper and it makes a big difference to the fly which side it chooses.

At one time, tax-free benefits were available only to the well-to-do because any purchase of municipal bonds under $25,000 was considered an "odd-lot" amount and would cost you extra brokerage commissions (as well as being harder to sell later). Under these conditions, the municipal bond market was strictly a high-priced investor's playground, and the cost of establishing a diversified portfolio of many municipal bonds was extraordinarily high. It was to remedy this situation that the municipal bond unit trust and the municipal bond mutual fund were developed.

What Are Municipal Funds and Trusts?

In some ways, the municipal bond unit trust and the municipal bond mutual fund are similar. Both offer a way for the small investor to buy a portion of a diversified selection of municipal bonds for as little as $1000. Both offer investments that are free of federal income taxes and, in some cases, state and local taxes (if you live in the state in which the bonds were issued). Also, both pay interest on a monthly basis, unlike the municipal bonds themselves, which pay interest only semiannually.

However, there are many differences between the unit trust and the mutual fund. Let's explore these differences so that you can decide which of the two might be worth considering as an investment for you.

How Does the Unit Trust Work?

A municipal bond unit trust is established by a sponsor who purchases a substantial share in at least 10, but more often 20 or more, long-term bond issues, usually with maturities ranging from 10 to 30 years. The bonds bought by the trust are left intact and do not change once they have been purchased. Therefore, the yield of the trust remains the same throughout its life span, which has a predetermined length that ends when the bonds in the portfolio mature. When you buy a share in a unit trust, you are buying a portion of this fixed portfolio, and you can predict just how long your investment will last and how much it will pay each year.

There are many types of unit trusts, and they vary greatly in terms of their length of maturity, degree of risk, tax-exempt status, and yield. The chances are excellent that you can find a trust with the right combination of features for your investment needs. You can buy units in a trust either directly, from the sponsoring firm, or indirectly, through your broker. It pays to work through your broker, who can offer you trusts assembled not only by his or her own firm but by other companies as well.

Once all the units in a particular trust have been sold, no more can be issued. You can dispose of your units without incurring a penalty or sales charge by asking your broker or the sponsoring firm to redeem them. In most cases, unit trust sponsors constitute a secondary market for their own units, and will guarantee to buy back your units at their current market value. Of course, this may or may not represent the same amount as you originally paid. If interest rates have risen since the trust was assembled, the rate being paid by the trust may no longer be competitive, and the market value of the units will be less than what you paid for them. On the other hand, if interest rates have fallen, you may make a profit when you sell your shares.

Because the portfolio of a unit trust is basically fixed, "managing" the trust is very simple. Therefore, a very small management fee is normally charged. However, when you purchase units in the trust, you must pay a commission which ranges from 2 to 5½ percent, depending on the company sponsoring the trust, the length of maturity, and other factors.

What would happen if one of the bonds in the trust should run into financial difficulties? Normally, the trustee may decide to sell that specific issue in the trust; however, unlike fund managers, trust managers are not permitted to add any new issues to their portfolios after they have been created. This tends to make trusts slower to respond when a bond's creditworthiness is in doubt. Also bear in mind the risk of early redemption. Many new issues are callable, meaning that the bonds can be called back after a specified period of time. This may occur if interest rates fall by more than 2 percentage points, so beware of high yield projections. Every trust prospectus must inform you of which bonds in its portfolio are subject to call and their dates of possible callability.

How Does the Municipal Fund Work?

A municipal bond mutual fund is similar to a money market fund: Its shares are highly liquid. Each fund sells or redeems shares at its net-asset value at any time, with some funds permitting redemption by wire transfer and even allowing investors to move from one fund to another by telephone. Whereas a bond unit trust stands pat with its investments, the managers of a bond fund are constantly trading. Thus the fund as a whole never matures but goes on indefinitely buying and selling bonds to take advantage of changes in the marketplace. Because of this continuous activity, a higher management fee, compared with that of the trust, is charged, usually about ½ percent annually.

Participation in a bond fund usually requires an initial investment of $1000. Any time thereafter you can buy additional shares in the fund. You have the option of receiving a check for your monthly earnings or having them automatically reinvested to purchase additional shares in the fund. Whenever you wish, you can sell your shares back to the fund. However, since the value of the bonds in the fund's portfolio fluctuates over time, you may or may not get back your original investment when you sell your shares.

How Does Insurance Affect the Trust or Fund?

Insured unit trusts and funds are normally not a good value, as the trust or fund is formed around many individual units, not just one bond. For example, a trust having 15 bonds that saw one of its bonds lose all its money would suffer a loss of only 6.6 percent. Since the cost of insurance over a 10-year period averages about 3 percent, you can see that you pay an extremely large premium to protect yourself from a minor loss. You're gambling on about 100-to-1 odds.

What Are the Basic Differences between the Trust and the Fund?

The differences between the municipal bond unit trust and the municipal bond mutual fund are summarized in Table 13.1.

If you're not sure whether a unit trust or a mutual fund is a

TABLE 13.1. THE MUNICIPAL BOND TRUST AND FUND COMPARED

	Unit trust	Mutual fund
Yield	Fixed	Varies with market conditions
Life of investment	Ends when bonds mature	Unending; constantly changing portfolio
Average maturity of bonds held	10–30 years	3 years or less
Purchase	Fixed number of units offered	Shares always available for purchase
Portfolio	Same bonds (15–20 issues) held to maturity	100 or more bonds actively managed
Disposal	Units sold through brokers like stock	Shares sold back to fund

better investment for you, follow this rule of thumb: The unit trust is a better choice if you are certain that you want to hold onto the investment for at least 5 years. If you think you may need to liquidate your holdings sooner than that—or if you anticipate shifting to other investments fairly frequently—the mutual fund is preferable. Either investment, however, is a good way for the small to medium-sized investor to get into municipal bonds with a diversified, professionally selected, tax-free portfolio of holdings.

However, you should be aware of how interest-sensitive municipals are. In times of stable interest rates, their after-tax yields are better than most investments (for the high-tax-bracket investor), and should interest rates decline, they can add capital gains also. It is when rates move upward that the bonds may become a problem because capital losses can occur upon their sale. Another problem that funds and trusts are currently experiencing involve two distinct areas: (1) the questionable quality of the bonds bought by funds and trusts looking to boost their yields, and (2) the threat that bond-rating agencies might lower the grades on many munis because of the ever-growing financial strains that may cripple state and local governments. Therefore, a word of caution. Look toward safety when considering muni funds or trusts, staying only with those funds that invest at least 90 percent of their portfolio in A or better rated bonds. You can get this information from the company's annual report, ask the salesperson, or write to the company. Also, bear in mind that the tax-free status of municipals affects individual retirees with a total modified adjusted gross income greater than $25,000 and couples with an income greater than $32,000, as they must pay taxes on a portion of their social security income. For the purposes of this computation, modified adjusted gross income includes tax-free municipal bond income, thus diminishing the value of the tax-exempt status of municipal bonds, trusts, or funds for retired people.

I have attempted in Chapters 12 and 13 to explain the concepts of municipal bonds, trusts, and funds. The lower marginal tax rates that we are now experiencing might seem to neutralize the main advantage of such issues. But, remember, it is a double-edged sword. While tax rates have fallen, many of the deductions and shelters have been partially or fully eliminated, thereby leading to increased rather than decreased taxes. Also, if Congress raises income taxes to offset the huge deficit, or if it extends limitations on issuers of municipal bonds (in other words, cuts the supply), the value of present-day municipals will rise greatly. When you compare them to taxable investment yields in Table 13.2, you can see why the municipals, whether they be in the form of bonds, trusts, or funds, represent a viable financial instrument in the money world today.

And on the topic of taxes, form 1040, the tax return we all file, could just as easily have been numbered 1039 or 1041. The IRS has assured the American public that the number

TABLE 13.2. TAXABLE INVESTMENT YIELD BEFORE AND AFTER TAX CONSIDERATION

Taxable investment yield, %	After federal and state tax deducted,* %
7.0	4.2
7.5	4.5
8.0	4.8
8.5	5.1
9.0	5.4
9.5	5.7
10.0	6.0
10.5	6.3
11.0	6.6
11.5	6.9
12	7.2

*Assumed combined tax, 40 percent.

1040 was a random selection. Still, some taxpayers insist it's not a mere coincidence that in Coventry, England, Lady Godiva, covered only by her long hair, rode naked through the streets protesting the high, oppressive taxes imposed by her husband, the Earl of Coventry, in the year 1040.

14

lutual Funds—
Spreading the Risk

*I am not so concerned with the return on my
investment as I am with the return of my
investment.*

Since October 1987, we have experienced stock market
plunges and record-breaking rises that today are still causing
anxiety among investors. If you still feel uncertain about the
market but would like to take some active part, a mutual fund
may be ideal.

How Does the Mutual Fund Work?

A large number of investors put their money together in a
pool to be managed by knowledgeable investment profes-
sionals. The price of a share in the mutual fund is determined
by the value of the fund's holdings. As the value of the stocks
owned by the fund increases, the share price increases and
the investors make a profit; if the value of the stocks decreases, the investors' shares are worth less and they suffer a
loss. The price of a share in a mutual fund (determined by dividing the net value of the fund's assets by the number of
shares outstanding) is usually announced once or twice a day.
The mutual fund also earns dividends that may be paid di-

rectly to investors or reinvested to buy additional shares in the fund.

Therefore, mutual funds can make money for their investors in three distinct ways:

1. The shareholders receive dividends earned through the investments that the fund possesses.

2. If a security in the fund's portfolio is sold at a profit, a capital gains distribution will be made by the fund to its shareholders.

3. If the value of the fund's portfolio increases, the value of each share also increases.

Mutual funds are normally created and managed by brokerage houses. As you'll learn, there are many kinds of mutual funds, depending on the types of stocks invested in, the degree of risk involved, the financial goals of the fund, etc. In choosing a fund for your own investment, there's a definite advantage to investing in a fund which is part of a "family of funds." This is a group of mutual funds with differing investment objectives managed by the same company that allows you to move your money from one fund to another (by written notification or by telephone), thus offering you maximum flexibility with a minimum of paperwork and lost time.

What Are the Advantages of Mutual Fund Ownership?

Mutual funds offer 10 important benefits to prospective stock market investors:

1. *Diversification and risk control:* Money invested in a mutual fund is used to buy shares in many different stock issues. This reduces your investment risk, since the failure of one or two companies out of many will not have a devastating effect on your portfolio. It would be impossible for an individual investor to achieve a comparable degree of diversification without having a very large sum to

invest in a variety of stocks. Also, with a small investment amount, you will find that by "doing it yourself" your transaction costs (commissions) will be very high because you will be transacting in small dollar amounts. Remember that diversification takes both time and a great deal of knowledge. And one more point: in the prospectus, the terms *diversified* or *nondiversified* may be used. A diversified fund must have at least 75 percent of its total portfolio in different securities so that no one investment can make up more than 5 percent of the fund's total assets. In a nondiversified fund, the requirement is reduced from 75 to 50 percent. However, as important as diversification is, the concept that stock funds shield you from stock market plunges is not always true. Even though there is a good amount of diversification (many different stocks in the same fund), if the market should tumble (as in 1987 and 1989) or fluctuate (as in the huge market swings in 1990 and 1991), diluting the risk by spreading your portfolio among many different stocks does nothing when virtually every issue falls.

2. *Professional management:* Few investors have the time, energy, or expertise to keep track of all the many factors affecting the stock market, including changes in interest rates and the money supply, new developments in technology, legal and political developments, foreign competition, and so on. Mutual fund companies have the resources to monitor these developments, for they employ staffs of researchers whose sole task is to keep track of business and economic trends that may affect the performance of stocks in the fund's portfolio. This expertise works to your benefit when you invest in the fund.

3. *Moderate cost:* Many mutual funds require only a small initial investment, with management fees averaging about ½ percent of your investment annually. By buying or selling in large blocks, the mutual fund pays a brokerage commission that is but a fraction of what you, the small investor, might have to pay. Also, certain types of securities should be bought only in large amounts. For ex-

ample, Treasury bonds produce the best prices on trades of $1 million or higher, far more than most of us can afford, but such trades are no problem for the mutual fund. For more information, see the discussion of load and no-load funds in the section on costs starting on page 110.

4. *Performance:* On balance, mutual funds have kept pace with the stock market as a whole. They have earned good returns in "bull" (rising) markets and have shown only small losses in "bear" (declining) markets.

5. *Fund-swapping option:* Many investment firms sponsor more than one type of mutual fund. The firms usually allow their investors to move money from one fund to another by means of letter or phone call. This is a convenient way to take advantage of changing investment conditions.

6. *Automatic deposits:* You can usually arrange for automatic investments to be made in your mutual fund account by specifying a dollar amount to be withdrawn from your bank account on a regular basis. This provides a painless way of building your investment portfolio month by month.

7. *Automatic reinvestment:* You can have all dividends, interest, and capital gains earned by your investment automatically reinvested in additional shares in the fund, another painless way of keeping your investment growing.

8. *Ease of withdrawal:* You can usually withdraw your funds by means of a letter authorizing the redemption of shares. You'll normally receive your money within 7 days.

9. *Reduction of record keeping:* The fund handles all stock transactions for you, records any changes in your holdings, and provides periodic statements showing all transactions, dividend distributions, reinvestments, and capital gains.

10. *Life insurance availability:* You can buy life insurance to cover your investment. If you designate a beneficiary by

means of a trust agreement, your invested funds will go directly to the beneficiary upon your death without incurring the costs or delays involved in the probate process.

What Are the Different Types of Mutual Funds?

Depending on your financial circumstances and your investment objectives, there are many types of mutual funds from which to choose. Let's consider the features of the most common types of funds:

Common stock fund: This fund invests in common stocks issued by corporations. Stock funds are often classified as either growth funds (holding riskier stocks that may pay low or no dividends but are expected to rise in value rapidly) or income funds (holding low-risk stocks that pay higher dividends but rise in value slowly).

Bond fund: This type invests in corporate or government bonds. Bond funds fall into several categories. High-grade bond funds deal in top-rated bonds with a high degree of safety and modest yields. Speculative bond funds deal in somewhat riskier bonds with ratings in the high B's that often pay higher yields. Junk bond funds carry both the greatest degree of risk and the greatest potential yield. But recently they have come under great pressure because of the losses they have incurred. And municipal bond funds invest in tax-free bonds issued by state and local governments and government agencies.

Balanced fund: A balanced fund holds shares in a combination of common stocks, preferred stocks, and bonds.

Industry fund: Such a fund invests in stocks issued by companies in a specific industry—energy, high technology, and public utilities, for example.

As your investment needs change over time, so do the types of funds which are best for you. When you are young, growth funds are usually best. Your financial needs are often modest at this time, and you can afford to take on a higher degree of risk in exchange for maximum growth potential. As you and your family grow older, diversification among various types of funds is desirable. Both stock funds and bond funds belong in your portfolio in middle age. When you near retirement age, current income becomes paramount. Bond funds are probably your best choice at this point. And investors of any age who find themselves in a high tax bracket should consider one of the tax-free funds which invest in municipal bonds or other tax-free investments.

What Are the Costs of Owning a Mutual Fund?

Depending on how they are purchased, mutual funds can be classified as either load or no-load funds. Let's look at the difference.

There are people who use self-service gas pumps and there are those who prefer service; the same goes for mutual funds. If you are not certain as to your current income needs, your risk involvement, and/or the price fluctuations of market investments, or if you simply don't have the time to be "involved," then the load fund is for you.

Shares in a *load fund* are sold through a stockbroker, who charges a sales commission that normally is about 6 percent of the purchase price (this is the *front load*). This commission, about three-quarters of which is kept by your individual broker while the balance goes to the sponsor of the fund, is deducted from your account before any investment is made. If you deposit $10,000 in a mutual fund that charges a load of 6 percent, only $9400 will actually be invested in the fund. Depending on the performance of the fund, it could take several months to a year to recoup the $600 commission. However, if you plan to remain in the fund for a number of years, the initial sales charge will become relatively unimportant over time. An annual management fee of about ½ percent of your investment is usually also charged.

What does your commission fee pay for? Primarily you are paying for the advice and services provided by your broker. As an investment professional, he or she should help you select the best fund or funds for your purposes and should keep you continually informed as to when you should move in or out of a particular instrument. If your broker doesn't provide this kind of expert advice, consider changing brokers; after all, you're paying for it.

No-load funds are usually sold through the mail by means of advertisements in newspapers or magazines. No sales broker is involved; therefore, no up-front commission must be paid. However, a service charge is levied each year. Also, you may have to pay an exit or redemption fee (rear-end load) when you withdraw from the fund. No sales advice or investment services are offered with a no-load fund. For detailed information on no-loads, write to No-Load Mutual Fund Association, P.O. Box 20C, Department 5, JAF Building, New York, New York 10016, and ask for the NLMFA reserve list. It is free.

In the past, no-load funds have included no commission fees because their shares were bought directly from the funds and not through the brokers. But, recently, funds have been imposing sales and distribution charges without the investor noticing them. These new "no-load funds" have what are called distribution fees which cover the cost of commissions in the same manner as front loads. Also, some of these funds have redemption fees that you will be charged if you redeem your holdings within the first few years, starting around 6 percent and declining to zero in about 6 years.

Are you aware that the no-load funds are allowed to have these fees because of a little-known regulation? Adopted in 1980 and permitted by the Securities and Exchange Commission (SEC), the regulation allows mutual no-load funds to annually charge (assess) shareholders an amount for advertising and direct market costs (mailing and prospectus) as well as for sales commissions. This is known as a "12b-1" charge.

What should you look for with a fund that charges 12b-1 fees? Look at the fund's financial statements and see if the 12b-1 charges are more than ¼ percent of the fund's assets. If they are, look for another fund, as the charges are excessive. Up until 1989 funds could hide these 12b-1 costs by scattering them throughout the entire prospectus (a booklet containing information to help evaluate the investment being offered), thereby hiding the fund's true cost. In 1989 the SEC enacted new rules that require the funds to disclose all fees and expenses in one table near the front of the prospectus. This table must show all expenses (both direct and indirect) paid by shareholders, and must also disclose the cumulative expenses paid on a $100 investment (5 percent return assumed at the end of 1-, 3-, 5-, and 10-year periods). In order to understand more about the instrument, remember the following poem, which I came upon years ago:

> Before you invest always read the prospectus.
> It's required by laws designed to protect us.
> Buried somewhere under mountains of prose
> Are all the risks to which you're exposed.
> So to understand the data, let me give you a hint.
> The greater the hazard, the smaller the print.

What Information Is Available?

And one final point regarding mutual funds. Each newspaper that carries daily information about the value of the funds may list data in different ways. Figure 14.1 is a standard reading of mutual funds as listed in the financial section of your newspaper.

And on the topic of information and advice, I have noticed that when a person with money meets a person with experience, the person with the experience gets the money and the person with the money gets the experience.

NAME	NAV	BUY	CHANGE
Joy Fund p	12.38	13.15	+.04
Happy Fund r	6.48	6.96	−.03
Smiley Fund t	18.86	19.09	−.12
Glad Fund	11.64	N.L.	+.19

Explanations

NAV (bid): Net asset value per share (in dollars and cents).

BUY (ask): Price paid by investors plus commission.

CHANGE: Change in NAV from yesterday.

Symbols

p: Fund imposes a 12b-1 charge.

r: Fund imposes a back-end fee (redemption price).

t: Used when both p and r are applied.

N.L.:   Signifies no front- or back-end load.

Figure 14.1 Sample mutual fund listing.

15

Real Estate as Security and Investment

A lot of homeowners have discovered that trees grow on money.

The real estate market has certainly cooled down since its fantastic rise in the decade of the 1980s. But now we are in the nineties and the future of real estate investment is in question. However, regardless of economic conditions, there are certain basic concepts that should be understood.

What Are the Benefits of Real Estate?

When you buy real estate for use as rental property, you can benefit by the purchase in at least three ways: It provides current income; it provides tax benefits through business expense deductions and depreciation; and, if you like, it can provide a place to live when you retire.

Let's consider first the tax benefits which result from offering property you own for rental purposes. First, any expenses you incur in operating the rental property are deductible from your income as business expenses. These might include repair and maintenance of the house or other property, interest payments on a mortgage, or an occasional trip to inspect the property if it is outside your own residential area.

Second, depreciation can be deducted from your income as well. This is the annual decline in value of any property which results from its increasing age. Depreciation is determined according to a fixed schedule depending on the nature of the property; a house, for example, is usually assumed to have a depreciable life of 27.5 years, so that you can deduct from your income a specified percentage of the house each year over a 27.5-year period. This is a noncash deduction, since you are not actually expending any money; yet you reap tax benefits just as if you were.

Interestingly, real estate values usually increase each year rather than decrease, despite what happens in a "soft" market. Therefore, you could say that you benefit twice: The actual resale value of your real property will generally grow, while you get a tax deduction because of the theoretical decrease in the value of your property over time.

Real estate, then, offers decided advantages to the canny investor. But like any other investment, it carries risks as well. The greatest is the risk of buying a property whose rental or resale value is minimal. It has been said that the three most important rules of real estate investment are location, location, and location, and that advice is pretty sound. There's no substitute for knowing the property and its actual value well. Never buy property you haven't personally visited and inspected. Photos or videotapes shown by an agent are no substitute; you'll never see the drawbacks of the property in that way. There are plenty of places in the world where no one is living and where no one will ever want to live. If you buy one of them, your chance of renting or selling the property is small, and mortgage payments, taxes, and other expenses will still have to be met. So above all, make sure you know the property before you buy.

What Rules Govern Investing in Real Estate?

1. Never buy property solely for its depreciation value. If a piece of real estate isn't a good investment in its own right, its tax benefits will not make it worthwhile.

2. Don't buy commercial property if you're a beginner in real estate investing. Single homes and small apartment houses are safer investments and more reliable sources of income.

3. Buy property within your own community, where you know property values and can anticipate trends. Your chance of success in the real estate field decreases as the distance from your home base increases.

4. Use as little cash as possible when buying real estate for investment purposes. Make a small down payment and take out the largest fixed-rate mortgage you can afford.

5. Don't invest in real estate unless you can reasonably foresee an annual profit from your investment (after deducting expenses and taxes) of at least 15 percent. The property itself should have a reasonable prospect for appreciation of about 10 percent annually.

6. Remember that renting can mean headaches for you as a landlord. The property must be maintained according to health and safety standards set by local governments, and complaints from tenants can be annoying. You might consider having a professional manager operate your property, but his or her fee, ranging from 6 to 10 percent of the rent, will cut heavily into your profit.

Is There an Alternative to a Direct Real Estate Purchase?

If you're interested in real estate investment but somewhat hesitant to get involved directly, consider a real estate investment trust (REIT). Like a mutual fund, a REIT pools money from many investors who buy shares in the trust's portfolio. However, rather than investing in stocks or bonds, a REIT invests in real estate.

Purchasing a REIT could be looked at as investing your money in real estate by the share instead of by the brick. When you receive shares in a trust, you are buying a stock that trades on a stock exchange just as any other stock does. Income from rent or interest on the mortgages is paid as dividends to the shareholders. These securities are required by law to pass 95 percent of the income they generate to shareholders in the form of dividends. When the property is sold, capital gains will be given to the stockholders as a special dividend or the sale may increase the earnings per share, thus raising the value of the stock. REIT investments fall into two basic categories:

1. *Equity:* This type of trust should be chosen if you feel that there will be high inflation. Remember that the higher the inflation, the greater the chance that your property values will increase and rents will rise.

2. *Mortgage:* If you feel that inflation will remain low, then the mortgage REITs' yields will look very attractive against a background of stable or even falling interest rates. All REITs, like bonds, rise in value when interest rates fall as investors run to higher-yielding securities. But because they are highly leveraged, these mortgage REITs will react much more intensely to interest rate movements than the equity REITs. For example, when rates fell sharply following the bloated years of 1980 to 1981 (15.75 percent in 1981 to 11.5 percent in 1982), mortgage REITs climbed an average of 44.6 percent compared with the equity REITs' 20.4 percent gain.

REITs have a number of advantages for investors. They allow small investors to participate in real estate investments that would otherwise be unavailable. Shares in a REIT are fairly liquid and can normally be sold at or near their full

value. They are a liquid method of owning what is traditionally an illiquid asset.

Naturally, REITs have their disadvantages. Management
and operating fees are charges which reduce the net earnings
of the trust and the amount of investor distributions as well.
The tax benefits normally associated with real estate ownership—including deductions for depreciation, interest, and
maintenance costs—are absorbed by the trust rather than
passed on to individual investors. REITs normally do not have
to pay taxes. However, you, the investor, do, as most dividends
received from these trusts are taxable at regular rates. There
is an exception. Dividends paid out of shareholders' equity
(which represents a return of capital) are not taxable. Also,
remember that any loss occurring from your REIT can be
used to offset capital gains you made during the year. Any loss
over gain can be deducted from your income for up to $3000
annually. And one last point: REITs do not always get the best
real estate choices, as many of the smaller REITs have trouble
competing with real estate syndicates, insurance companies,
and large pension funds for properties.

What Are the Tax Benefits of Selling a Home?

Before ending the topic of real estate investments, let's examine one other aspect: the selling of your home and its tax ram-
ifications. When you sell your home and a profit is realized,
you will get two favorable tax treatments:

1. You will be able to postpone the tax on the profit indefinitely if you purchase another primary residence within 2
   years.

2. If you are over age 55, you may take a one-time capital-
   gains exclusion of $125,000 against the profit from the
   sale of the home. This exclusion can include untaxed
   profits on previous homes so long as the total does not exceed $125,000. You will qualify for this exclusion if:

- You are 55 or older.
- You own and have occupied the home as your primary residence for at least 3 of the last 5 years before the sale. This 3-year occupancy rule may be accumulated with temporary absences during the 5-year period. Even if you rent, as long as it is not more than 2 years (during the 5-year period), the renting will not hurt your ability to use the $125,000 exclusion.
- Neither you nor your spouse has ever taken this exclusion before.

You can get more information by writing to the IRS for a free copy of Publication 523, "Tax Information on Selling Your Home," or calling 1-800-829-3676.

Over the past 2 decades, real estate values in the United States have soared, with few other investments showing such a comparable growth. If the U.S. economy continues to prosper, real estate will continue to benefit. As long as you know what you're buying, the chances are that you can do very well by investing in real estate. And on the topic of real estate, by the time you finish paying for a house in the country, it's no longer the country.

16

Stock Market—Bulls, Bears, and Pigs

In the bust of 1987, I made a killing in the market. I shot my broker.

Just prior to October 19, 1987, everyone was witnessing a major surge in the stock market. Money was being made everywhere and the golden bubble of prosperity just grew and grew. Then came the inevitable burst in 1987 and again in 1989. It is said that bulls can make money and bears can make money, but pigs get slaughtered. And that is exactly what happened.

There's no doubt that investing in the stock market can be one of the most exciting ways of making money. Nothing quite compares with the thrill of seeing the little-known stock you picked become a hot property, perhaps doubling in price—and then doubling again and again. But as with any investment, the potential risks are equal to the rewards. Middle-income investors who want to play the market owe it to themselves to become fully informed before getting involved. This chapter should be only the beginning of a continuing process of education for anyone interested in becoming a successful stock market investor.

How Does the Stock Market Work?

A share of stock represents a unit of ownership in a corporation. When you buy stock, you are becoming a part-owner of the business. Therefore, you benefit from any increase in the value of the corporation, and you suffer when the corporation performs badly. You're also entitled to share in the profits earned by the corporation.

Stocks are bought and sold in marketplaces known as *stock exchanges.* The exchange itself does not buy or sell stock, nor does it set the price of stock; the exchange is simply a forum in which individuals and institutions may trade in stocks. Stock exchanges play a vital role in a capitalist economy. They provide a way for individuals to purchase shares in thousands of businesses, and they provide businesses with an important source of capital for expansion, growth, research, and development.

There are two types of stock exchanges: organized and unorganized.

There are some 14 organized stock exchanges currently operating in the United States, of which the New York Stock Exchange (NYSE) is both the best known and the largest (over 1300 members). Only members may trade shares on a stock exchange, and only individuals may become members, although a member may be a partner or an officer in a brokerage firm (known as a *member firm*). To become a member, you must buy a membership, or "seat," from another member or from an estate. The price of a seat varies greatly, depending on the volume of business being transacted. A seat on the NYSE within the last 20 years has sold for as little as $35,000 (in 1977) to as much as $1,150,000 (in 1987).

Most brokerage firms own seats on an exchange, with one of the firm's officers designated as a member. In their role as brokers, members carry out clients' orders to buy or sell certificates on the floor of the exchange. In communication with other exchange members, brokers can carry out buy-and-sell transactions right on the exchange floor. Current sale prices on each stock being traded are constantly updated and made available to all members. Thus the exchange operates as a kind of auction market for the trading of securities.

How Does an Investor Purchase Stock?

Here's what happens when an investor decides to buy or sell a particular stock.

First, an account executive at the brokerage house receives the buy or sell order, which may take any of several forms:

Round lot order: An order to buy or sell 100 shares, considered the standard trading unit

Odd lot order: An order to buy or sell fewer than 100 shares

Market order: An order to buy or sell at the best available price

Limit order: An order to buy or sell at a specified price

Stop order: An order designed to protect profits or limit losses by calling for sale of stock when its price falls to a specified level

Good till canceled (GTC) order: An order that remains open until it is executed or canceled by the investor

Second, after the order is received, it is sent by teletype to the floor of the stock exchange. The brokerage firm's floor broker receives the order and executes it at the appropriate trading post. Confirmation of the transaction is teletyped back to the account executive at the local office, who notifies the investor. Remarkably, the entire process may take as little as 2 or 3 minutes.

Not all stocks are traded on any of the 14 organized exchanges. Those that are not are traded "over the counter" in the so-called unorganized exchange. Not a physical place, the unorganized exchange consists of thousands of brokers and dealers who trade in about 50,000 different unlisted stocks through telephone or telegraph communication. A computer system, known as the National Association of Security

Dealers Automated Quotation System (NASDAQ), is used to provide instant bid and asked prices on stocks.

In the over-the-counter market, transactions are negotiated privately rather than on an auction basis. An investor wishing to purchase a particular unlisted security consults a broker, who contacts other brokers dealing in that stock. The broker offering the stock for sale at the lowest price receives the offer.

Prices of over-the-counter stocks are quoted as both bid and asked prices. The bid price is the final price offered by a buyer, while the asked price is the final price requested by a seller. Trades are normally made when the bid and asked prices approach one another.

What Kinds of Stocks Are Available?

There are two kinds of stocks: common and preferred.

What Is Common Stock and What Investment Strategies Are Associated with It?

A share of common stock represents a unit of ownership, or "equity," in the issuing corporation. Each share of common stock usually bears a par value, which is a more or less arbitrary value established in the corporation's charter and bearing little relation to the stock's actual market value. The market value is influenced by many factors, including the corporation's potential earning power, its financial condition, its earning record, its record for paying dividends, and general business conditions.

Ownership of a share of common stock carries certain privileges:

1. *A share in earnings:* Each year, the board of directors of the corporation meets to determine the amount of the corporation's earnings that will be distributed to stockholders. This distribution, known as the *dividend,* will vary

depending on the company's current profitability. It may be omitted altogether if the company is earning no current profits or if the board elects to plow back profits into growth.

2. *A share in control:* Holders of common stock have the right to vote on matters of corporate policy on the basis of one vote per share held. However, the small investor with only a few shares of stock has little or no practical influence on corporate decisions.

3. *A claim on assets:* In the event of the company's liquidation, holders of common stock have the right to share in the firm's assets after all debts and prior claims have been satisfied.

There are four main categories of common stocks, each of which is best for a particular investment strategy and purpose.

1. *Blue-chip stocks:* High-grade, or blue-chip, stocks are issued by well-established corporations with many years of proven success, earnings growth, and consistent dividend payments. Blue-chip stocks tend to be relatively high priced and offer a relatively low income yield. However, they are a very safe investment, but is that your most important concern? Remember, a ship in the harbor is safe, but is that what ships are built for?

2. *Income stocks:* Income stocks pay a higher-than-average return on investment. They are generally issued by firms in stable businesses which have no need to reinvest a large percentage of profits each year.

3. *Growth stocks:* Issued by firms expected to grow rapidly during the years to come, growth stocks have a current income that is often low, since the company plows back most earnings into research and expansion. However, the value of the stock may rise quickly if the company performs up to expectations.

4. *Speculative stocks:* Speculative stocks are backed by no proven corporate track record or lengthy dividend his-

tory. Stocks issued by little-known companies or newly formed corporations, high-flying "glamour" stocks issued by companies in new business areas, and low-priced "penny stocks" may all be considered speculative stocks. As with any speculative investment, there is a possibility of tremendous profit—but a substantial risk of losing all as well.

What Are the Differences between Preferred and Common Stock?

Preferred stock, like common stock, represents ownership of a share in a corporation. However, holders of preferred stock have a prior claim on the company's earnings as compared with holders of common stock; hence the name *preferred stock.* Similarly, holders of preferred stock have a prior claim on the company's assets in the event of a liquidation.

Preferred stock also has certain distinctive features related to dividend payments. A fixed, prespecified annual dividend is usually paid for each share of preferred stock. This fixed dividend may be expressed in dollars (for example, $10 per share) or as a percentage of the stock's par value. It must be paid before dividends are issued to holders of common stock.

However, preferred stock dividends are not considered a debt of the corporation—unlike, for example, the interest due on corporate bonds—because the firm is not obligated to meet its dividend payments. If the corporation is losing money, the board of directors may decide to withhold the dividend payment for a given year. To protect stockholders against undue losses, most preferred stock is issued with a cumulative feature. If a dividend is not paid on cumulative preferred stock, the amount is carried over to the following period, and both dividends must be paid before holders of common stock can receive any dividend.

Some preferred stocks are convertible. This means that shares of preferred stock can be exchanged for shares of common stock issued by the same company. Prices of convertible preferred stocks tend to vary more than those of other preferred stocks, since they are affected by changes in the prices of the corresponding common stocks.

Unlike common stock, preferred stock carries no voting privileges. Most of the stock issued in the United States is of the common, rather than the preferred, variety.

What Are the Advantages and Disadvantages of Stocks?

Like any investment, stocks have distinct advantages and disadvantages. Some of these should have already become apparent. Let's take a systematic look at them. First, the advantages of investing in stocks:

Growth potential: When a company has the potential for growth in value and earnings, so does its stock. If you pick the right stock or group of stocks, you can profit significantly and relatively quickly. History shows that, as a whole, the stock market has had an upward trend in values, with years of gain outnumbering those of decline by better than 3 to 1.

Liquidity: Stocks traded on the major exchanges can be bought and sold quickly and easily at prices readily ascertained.

Possible tax benefits: Growth stocks, which pay low or no dividends so that company profits can be reinvested, provide an effective tax shelter for your profits. As the corporation's value grows, so does the value of your stock, which is a form of tax-deferred income, since no taxes need be paid on these gains until you sell the stock.

Now, the disadvantages:

Risk: There can be no guarantee that you will make money investing in stocks. Companies may fail, stock prices may drop, and you may lose your investment. Remember the saying of one concerned investor, "I am not so concerned with the return *on* my investment as I am with the return *of* my investment."

Brokerage commissions: Most investors need the help and advice of a stockbroker when involved in the market. However, high brokers' commissions can largely erode your profits. Since one fee is charged when you buy your stocks and another when you sell them, you are, in effect, forced to pay twice. If you're an unusually well-informed investor, consider one of the growing firms of discount brokers, which provide little or no investment counseling but charge greatly reduced commissions when trading your stocks.

Complexity: The stock market is a complicated subject, and the amount of knowledge needed to be consistently successful is tremendous. Investors who lack the patience, time, or skill to inform themselves about the market often buy and sell on impulse, thereby minimizing their profits and maximizing their losses. If you get into the stock market, be prepared to devote the time and work necessary to make intelligent decisions instead of haphazard ones.

And on the topic of stocks, what keeps most people out of the stock market is the supermarket.

17

Stock Market Information— Where to Get It

*It's not the bulls and the bears on Wall Street
that make you lose money, it's the bum steers.*

Now that you know the basic characteristics of the different kinds of stocks, let's take a look at some of the things you should know to get started in stock market investing.

How Do You Learn about Investing in the Stock Market?

An investor's most important tool is information: information about stock prices, movement in the market, and likely future business trends. Without plenty of sound information, investment decisions are pure guesswork. The first place to look for information about any stock is the financial pages of your newspaper, and the best place to start is with the columns listing the current stock prices on one or more of the major organized exchanges. Figures 17.1 and 17.2 provide explanations of the information you'll find in those columns and what it means for you as a prospective investor. The sample in Figure 17.1 shows a typical listing for a stock traded on one of the major exchanges.

High (1)	Low (1)	Stock (2)	Div (3)	P/E (4)	100s (5)	High (6)	Low (7)	Last (8)	Change (9)
44	16	XYZ	2.50	7	33	35¼	34	35	+½

(1) High and Low: These are the highest and lowest prices paid for the stock during the previous year (over 52 weeks). This entry shows that the highest price paid for XYZ stock during the previous year was $44 per share; the lowest price, $16 per share.

(2) Stock: Stocks are listed alphabetically by an abbreviated form of the corporate name.

(3) Dividend: The rate of annual dividend is shown; it is generally an estimate based on the previous quarterly or semiannual payment. This entry shows that XYZ is paying an annual dividend of $2.50 per share or about 7% (2.50 ÷ 35).

(4) Price/Earnings Ratio: This is the ratio of the market price of the stock to the annual earnings of the company per share of stock. As you'll learn later, this is an important indicator of corporate success and investor confidence.

(5) Shares Traded: This is the number of shares sold for the day, expressed in hundreds. In the example shown, 3300 shares of XYZ stock were traded. The figure does not include odd-lot sales. Note: if the number in this column is preceded by a "z," it signifies the actual number of shares traded, not hundreds.

(6) and (7) High and Low: These are the highest and lowest prices paid for XYZ stock during the trading session (that is, the business day). The highest price paid for XYZ stock was $35.25 per share; the lowest price, $34 per share. Stock prices are shown in dollars and fractions of dollars, ranging from ⅛ to ⅞.

(8) Closing Price: The final price of XYZ stock for the day. In this case, it was $35 per share.

(9) Change: The difference between the closing price of the stock for this session and the closing price for the previous session. Since XYZ stock closed at $35 per share, up ½ (or 50 cents) from the previous close, yesterday's closing price would have been $34.50.

Figure 17.1. Sample stock listing.

Newspapers can list only a small fraction of the thousands of stocks traded over the counter. Therefore, a phone call to your broker is a must if you are interested in the day's activity in a particular over-the-counter (OTC) stock.

Newspaper listings for OTC stocks are simpler than those for stocks traded on a major exchange (see Figure 17.2). A newspaper listing is a useful place to start in getting information and analyzing the value of a particular stock. However, it's only a starting place. Facts derived from a corporation's annual report, newspaper and magazine articles about the business, stock market newsletters and columnists' comments, and the advice of your broker can all be helpful. An old saying is very appropriate: "Buy on rumor, sell on news." Hearsay aside, facts are your most important asset.

Stock	Bid	Asked	Bid change
PENY	7¼	8¼	+¾

Stock: The abbreviated name of the issuing company.

Bid: This is the price at which dealers are willing to buy the stock; in this case, $7.25 per share.

Asked: This is the price at which dealers are willing to sell the stock; it is always higher than the bid price. In this case, it is $8.25 per share.

Bid Change: This is the difference between the bid price today and the bid price at the close of the previous day. Since today's bid price is up ¾ from the previous day's close, the bid price yesterday was $6.50 per share.

Figure 17.2. Sample OTC stock listing.

What Statistics Should You Know to Evaluate Stocks?

Certain statistics that are widely available for any listed stock can tell you a good deal about its investment prospects.

1. *Earnings per share:* The current earnings-per-share figure is one basic measure of the success of a corporation. It is computed by taking the corporation's net profit after taxes, subtracting any preferred stock dividends, and dividing the remainder by the number of outstanding shares of common stock. For example, suppose XYZ Corporation earned a net profit of $4,300,000 last year, paid a dividend on preferred stock of $300,000, and has 800,000 outstanding shares of common stock. The earnings per share for XYZ Corporation are $5:

$4,300,000	Net profit after taxes
– 300,000	Dividend on preferred stock
$4,000,000	
÷ 800,000	Outstanding shares of common stock
= $5	Earnings per share

2. *Book value:* This is one measure of the value of the assets of the corporation. It is computed by taking the listed value of the assets, subtracting amounts due to creditors and preferred stockholders, and dividing the remainder by the number of outstanding shares of common stock. To take another simple example, suppose XYZ Corporation owns assets valued at $30 million, has debts totaling $10 million, and has 800,000 shares of common stock outstanding. The book value of XYZ Corporation is $25 per share.

$30,000,000	Assets
– 10,000,000	Debts and value of preferred stock
$20,000,000	
÷ 800,000	Outstanding shares of common stock
= $25	Book value per share

3. *Price/earnings (P/E) ratio:* This important index allows you to compare the market price of the stock to its demonstrated earning power. A low P/E ratio—say, under 7— shows that the company has high earnings relative to the current market price of its stock and suggests that the market has undervalued the stock. The stock is probably a

good buy at its current price. Stocks with low price/earnings ratios can reward you in two ways:

- If they're undervalued, their prices should eventually go up.
- If the market as a whole slumps, they may not sink as much.

For cautious investors, low P/E ratio stocks make sense. A host of different studies have shown that, as a group, such stocks perform better, over the years, than a group with medium or high P/E ratios. Conversely, a high P/E ratio (15 or more) shows that the market expects large future gains from the company and has therefore driven up the price of the stock. The P/E ratio is computed by dividing the stock's market price by the company's earnings per share. If stock in GUK Corporation is selling at $35 per share and the company has earnings of $3 per share, the P/E ratio is 35 ÷ 3, or 11.6, which is a bit lower than the average P/E ratio of 13.

4. *Yield:* This figure offers another indication as to how reasonable the current price of a stock is. It is a percentage determined by dividing the current annual dividend per share by the current market price of a share. If XYZ Corporation is paying an annual dividend of $2.50 per share and the stock is selling at $35 per share, then the yield is 2.50 ÷ 35, or about 7.1 percent.

5. *Rate of return:* The rate of return on a given stock is a measure of the total profit you gain from holding that stock for a specified period of time. Computing the rate of return involves several steps. First, find the total market value of your stock at the end of the period in question. Add to this figure the total amount of dividends earned by the stock during the period. Divide this sum by the total market value of the stock at the start of the period. Subtract 1, and multiply by 100. The resulting figure, expressed as a percentage, is your rate of return for the period. Here's an example. Suppose you bought 100 shares of AJL stock at $24 per share. You've held the stock for 1 year. The stock paid a $2 per share dividend during the

course of the year. At the end of the year, it has a market value of $25 per share. The rate of return for this stock is 12.5 percent, calculated in this way:

$2500   Market value of stock at end of period
+   200   Dividend paid during period
$2700 ÷ 2400 = 1.125 (market value of stock at start
                    of period)

1.125 − 1.0 = 0.125 × 100 = 12.5% rate of return

Each of these five indicators—earnings per share, book value, price/earnings ratio, yield, and rate of return—is an important factor in judging the value of a stock offering.

What Is the Dow Jones Industrial Average?

In attempts to gauge or predict large-scale trends in stock market values, the Dow Jones Industrial Average (DJIA) is often cited. The most frequently mentioned of four Dow Jones Averages (covering industrial stocks, transportation stocks, utility stocks, and a composite average), the DJIA is a barometer of stock market trends based on prices of 30 large U.S. corporations listed on the NYSE. Every day, the fluctuations in the prices of these stocks are combined by adding up the prices of the 30 stocks and dividing the result by a designated factor (used to compensate for complicating situations, such as stock splits and periodic substitutions in the list of stocks used). The 30 stocks that made up the DJIA during 1991 are:

Alcoa	Caterpillar	General Electric
Allied Signal	Chevron	General Motors
American Express	Coca-Cola	Goodyear
AT&T	Du Pont	IBM
Bethlehem Steel	Eastman Kodak	International Paper
Boeing	Exxon	J. P. Morgan

McDonald's	Procter & Gamble	United Technologies
Merck	Sears, Roebuck	Walt Disney
Minnesota Mining	Texaco	Westinghouse
Philip Morris	Union Carbide	F. W. Woolworth

The DJIA has been widely criticized as an inaccurate reflection of the U.S. economy and U.S. stock market. The Dow is weighted with older, heavy manufacturing firms and doesn't fully measure the impact of newer, high-tech companies. The mathematical method used in calculating the Dow has also been attacked on various technical grounds. Other indexes, such as the Standard & Poor's Composite Index, which is based on prices of 500 stocks, have been created to compete with the Dow. Nonetheless, the Dow Jones Industrial Average remains the most popular and influential measurement of the direction and strength of the U.S. stock market.

In summary, the past few years since the turbulent changes of the late eighties have certainly put us on the road to recovery. Even the Persian Gulf War did not play havoc with the market, for new safeguards had been put in place. The NYSE has curbed program trading, and some brokerage houses have begun to pull in the reins of margin accounts. It is true that there is no way to tell where the market will be a year or two from now, but by keeping informed, you stand a better chance in this roller coaster market we are now all experiencing. And on the topic of the market, Wall Street is a place where the day begins with good buys.

18

Treasuries
Are a Treasure

If your ship doesn't come in, swim out to it.

The U.S. Treasury Department has one of the biggest jobs imaginable—providing money for the enormous financial needs of the federal government. No wonder the laws that are created are called "bills." Much of the money the Treasury raises comes from the sale of securities to the general public and institutional investors. These securities are known as *Treasury obligations* and consist of Treasury bills, notes, and bonds.

What Is the Best Method of Purchasing Treasury Obligations?

One way is to go to the secondary market and purchase them just as you would any stock or bond. However, this secondary market method does have a hidden transaction cost based on the bid/ask differential (known as the *spread*), to which a retail markup may also be added. I am not in favor of this method since it may not be worth the extra cost. A better method is by direct purchase, whether through commercial banks, brokerage houses, and other financial institutions, which charge a fee, or without a fee through any of the 12 Federal Reserve banks or one of their 24 branches. This Treasury purchase can be made by (1) mail postmarked no later than the day before the auction with the words "Tender for Treasury" on the bottom left side of the envelope or (2) in person by 12 p.m. Eastern Standard Time on the day of the auction. For specific information on Treasury bills, call (202) 287-4091; on Treasury notes and bonds, (202) 287-4088; and on Treasury prices and quotes, (202) 287-4400. A listing of the addresses and telephone numbers of the 12 Federal Reserve banks and 24 branch banks follows.

Alabama	P.O. Box 830447, Birmingham 35283, (205) 252-3141, Ext. 264
Arkansas	P.O. Box 1261, Little Rock 72203, (501) 372-5451, Ext. 288
California	P.O. Box 2077, Terminal Annex, Los Angeles 90051, (213) 683-2300
	P.O. Box 7702, San Francisco 94120, (415) 974-2330
Colorado	P.O. Box 5228, Terminal Annex, Denver 80217, (303) 572-2473 or 2470
District of Columbia	Board of Governors, Federal Reserve System, Washington, D.C. 20551, (202) 452-3244
Florida	P.O. Box 929, Jacksonville 32221, (904) 632-1000
	P.O. Box 520847, Miami 33152, (305) 591-2065
Georgia	104 Marietta St. N.W., Atlanta 30303, (404) 521-8653
Illinois	P.O. Box 834, Chicago 60690, (312) 322-5369
Kentucky	P.O. Box 32710, Louisville 40232, (502) 568-9236 or 9238
Louisiana	P.O. Box 61630, New Orleans 70161, (504) 586-1505, Ext. 293
Maryland	P.O. Box 1378, Baltimore 21203, (301) 576-3553
Massachusetts	P.O. Box 2076, Boston 02106, (617) 973-3805 or 3810
Michigan	P.O. Box 1059, Detroit 48231, (313) 964-6157 or 6158
Minnesota	250 Marquette Ave., Minneapolis 55480, (612) 340-2233
Missouri	P.O. Box 440, Kansas City 64141, (816) 881-2783 or 2409
	P.O. Box 14915, Attn.: Treasury Issues, St. Louis, (314) 444-8506
Nebraska	2201 Farnam St., Omaha 68102, (402) 221-5633
New York	P.O. Box 961, Buffalo 14240, (716) 849-5030
	33 Liberty St., New York City 10045, (212) 720-6619
No. Carolina	P.O. Box 30248, Charlotte 28230, (704) 336-7267
Ohio	P.O. Box 999, Cincinnati 45201, (513) 721-4787, Ext. 334
	P.O. Box 6387, Cleveland 44101, (216) 579-2490
Oklahoma	P.O. Box 25129, Oklahoma City 73125, (405) 270-8652

Oregon	P.O. Box 3436, Portland 97208, (503) 221-5932
Pennsylvania	P.O. Box 90, Philadelphia 19105, (215) 574-6680 or 6675
	P.O. Box 867, Pittsburgh 15230, (412) 261-7802
Tennessee	P.O. Box 407, Memphis 38101, (901) 523-7171, Ext. 622 or 629
	301 Eighth Ave. North, Nashville 37203, (615) 259-4006, Ext. 261
Texas	400 S. Akard St., Station K, Dallas 75222, (214) 651-6362
	P.O. Box 2578, Houston 77252, (713) 659-4433
	P.O. Box 1471, San Antonio 78295, (512) 224-2141, Ext. 305 or 309
Utah	P.O. Box 30780, Salt Lake City 84130, (801) 322-7844
Virginia	P.O. Box 27622, Richmond 23261, (804) 697-8372
Washington	P.O. Box 3567, Terminal Annex, Seattle 98104, (206) 442-1652

Treasury obligations are tax-exempt at the state and local levels and are backed by "the full faith and credit" of the United States. The credit risk involved in this form of investment is considered practically nil (despite what you may have heard about 12-digit federal deficits). In comparison with similar obligations issued by corporations, Treasury obligations usually pay a yield which is 1 or 2 percentage points lower. However, many people are willing to accept the slightly lower yield in exchange for absolute safety. As the saying goes, you can eat well or sleep well, but you can't do both.

When you buy a Treasury obligation, you can have its ownership registered in any of four ways:

Single owner: For example, Tom Green (social security number 100-10-1000).

Two owners: For example, Tom Green (100-10-1000) and Betty Green (200-20-2000).

Joint tenancy: For example, Tom Green (100-10-1000) or Betty Green (200-20-2000).

Guardian or custodian for a minor: For example, Betty Green, guardian (or custodian) for Tom Green, Jr. (300-30-3000).

Treasury obligations can't be registered solely in the name of a minor.

What Are Treasury Bills and How Do They Work?

Treasury bills, or T-bills, are issued with maturities of 3, 6, and 12 months and sold in minimum amounts of $10,000 and additional multiples of $5000. They are sold at discount (interest becomes yours immediately) and redeemed, upon maturity, at face value.

T-bills are sold at auction on a regular basis. It is at this auction that the interest rate to be paid is set, normally resulting from the competitive bids of large institutional investors. Auctions for 3- and 6-month bills are held every Monday, while auctions for 12-month bills are held every fourth Thursday.

If you buy your T-bill from a commercial bank or broker, you'll be charged a small fee (which is tax-deductible). If you buy your T-bill directly from the Federal Reserve, no fee is charged. Here's how to go about it.

Bring your payment for a T-bill in the denomination you prefer to the nearest branch of the Federal Reserve bank, making sure that it is received prior to 1 p.m. Eastern Standard Time on the day of the auction. The payment must be in the form of cash, a certified personal check, a bank check, or a matured U.S. Treasury note or bond, and it must be for the full face value of the T-bill. When the auction takes place, the interest rate for the bills sold that day is set, and the amount of the discount to which you are entitled is determined accordingly. You are then sent a check for the amount of the discount (see the discussion of Treasury direct on page 141). If no Federal Reserve bank is nearby, you can send for an application by writing either to the Bureau of the Public Debt, Division of Customer Services, or to your local Federal Reserve bank and request the booklet "Basic Information on Treasury Securities—Treasury Direct." If you do not have an application, you can send a letter with a certified check and the following information:

1. Your name, address, social security number, and daytime phone number.
2. A statement saying that your bid is noncompetitive.
3. The amount (face value) you wish to purchase.
4. The maturity of the bill (3-, 6-, or 12 months).
5. Your account number at your bank (for direct deposit).

Remember though, that you will lose the opportunity to earn interest during the period from the auction to the settlement date. If you buy your Treasury bill from a commercial bank, although there is a fee of about $50, you continue to earn interest on your money right up to the settlement date because the bank will not transfer your funds until that date.

Do You Receive a Certificate When You Purchase a T-Bill?

The sale of treasury bills is recorded in book-entry form, meaning that the Fed will not send you a certificate as it has done in the past. The securities are now held through the Federal Reserve records in a Treasury direct account that will be opened when you purchase the securities. Thereafter, all future Treasury transactions will be placed in that account when an order is placed on the tender form. By this book-entry method, you can reinvest the maturing Treasury principal automatically for up to 2 years (eight times for a 3-month bill, four times for a 6-month bill, and twice for a 1-year bill) before you need an investment renewal request. Also, remember that you must complete a W-9 (request for a taxpayer identification number) or a portion of your proceeds will be withheld for payment of income tax on your earnings.

When the maturity date of the T-bill arrives, you can re-deem the bill for its full face value. And since you received the interest (in the form of the discount) in advance, the yield is actually higher than the nominal interest rate.

How Is Interest Paid and What Are the Tax Consequences?

Suppose you buy a $10,000, 1-year T-bill with an interest rate set by auction at 7 percent. After paying your $10,000, you'll receive by mail (see the discussion of Treasury direct on page 141) a check for the 7 percent discount, or $700. Thus the ef-fective price of the T-bill is just $9300. Since you've now re-ceived $700 income on that $9300 investment, your true yield is 7.5 percent. To summarize:

1. $10,000 × 0.07 = $700. This is the discount sent to you.
2. $10,000 − $700 = $9300. This is your net cost.
3. $700 ÷ $9300 = 7.5%. This is your true yield on an annual basis.

And, of course, you're free to take the $700 and invest it somewhere else for the rest of the year, thus increasing your income further.

For federal income tax purposes, the $700 is considered or-dinary income to be reported at the time the T-bill matures, not at the time you receive it. For example, if you buy a 6-month T-bill in July 1991, you'll receive your full discount im-mediately. However, the amount of the discount is not consid-ered income until January 1992, when the T-bill matures. Therefore, it would not have to be declared for tax purposes, nor would taxes have to be paid on it until as late as April 1993. (Estimated tax is not considered in this example.)

What Happens at the Time of Maturity?

When it's time to redeem your T-bill, if you bought it through a bank or a broker, you'll follow the procedure arranged at the time of purchase. If you bought it directly from a Federal Reserve bank, the Treasury Department will make a direct deposit for you into your bank. This new program, known as *Treasury direct,* smooths the way for you by having the interest payments and proceeds (when the security matures) automatically deposited in your account at any bank of your choosing. If you are holding several issues, your portfolio will be merged into one master account. No certificates are given to you at purchase, but you will receive a receipt and an account statement. At redemption, you can also automatically roll over (reinvest) your funds in new T-bills by indicating this choice on form PD4633-2, which the Treasury Department sends to all holders of T-bills prior to maturity.

If for any reason you have to cash in your T-bill before it matures and you bought it at a Federal Reserve bank, it must first be transferred to a bank or broker who then sells it on the open market. You will need to obtain a securities transfer request (STR) and submit it to the bank from which you bought the T-bill. The amount of proceeds will vary from day to day because the maturity value of the bill is affected by (1) interest rates prevailing on the sale date, (2) the number of days remaining before the T-bill matures, and (3) the bank or brokerage fee.

What Are Treasury Notes?

Treasury notes, like T-bills, pay interest rates determined by auction. However, they are not sold at a discount. Instead they pay interest every 6 months at a rate fixed at the time of purchase. In this respect, they resemble corporate bonds.

Treasury notes also have a longer life span than T-bills (up to 10 years) from the date of issue. Notes that mature in less than 4 years are offered by the Treasury in minimum denominations of $5000, while those maturing in 4 years or longer are sold in minimum denominations of $1000. Treasury note auctions are held on the following schedule:

$5000 initially, $5000 increments	2-year	Monthly; on a Wednesday late in the month
	3-year	Quarterly; early in February, May, August, and November
$1000 initially, $1000 increments	4-year	Quarterly; late in March, June, September, and December
	5-year	Quarterly; late in February, May, August, and November
	7-year	Quarterly; early in January, April, July, and October
	10-year	Quarterly; early in February, May, August, and November

Like corporate bonds, Treasury notes can also be bought and sold on the secondary market by brokers and banks. The U.S. Treasury doesn't buy back Treasury notes; however, you can exchange notes of one denomination for those of another. The market price for a Treasury note will fluctuate, depending on changes in interest rates. You can find current prices in the financial pages of your newspaper. However, the actual price you'll pay a broker—or the amount you'll receive when selling your note—will differ from the price shown, because of the broker's fee and the slightly higher costs involved in buying or selling odd-lot amounts (which include any purchase of less than $1 million worth of Treasury notes).

What Are Treasury Bonds?

Treasury bonds are much like Treasury notes, with a few differences. They have longer maturity periods, ranging from 10 to 30 years. Treasury bonds with 10- and 30-year maturities are auctioned during February, May, August, and November, while 20-year bonds are auctioned during March, June, September, and December. The minimum investment is $1000, with bonds available in denominations of $1000, $5000, $10,000, $100,000, and $1,000,000. Treasury bonds tend to fluctuate in price on the secondary market more than Treasury notes, and so it is possible to lose on a Treasury obligation. Suppose that the $1000, 20-year Treasury bond you bought last year appears on your statement valued at only $970. What happened to the remaining $30? Nothing, really, as you will get back your $1000 at maturity, so no risk is involved. But there is a risk on the secondary market (where Treasury obligations are traded) if you decide to sell the bond before it matures in 20 years. The proceeds from the sale are based on the market value of the bond, which depends on the direction of interest rates. When these rates rise, bond prices will tend to decrease. For example, if you bought a 20-year, 8 percent Treasury bond for $1000 today and in 3 years interest rates should rise to 10 percent, the market value of your T-bond would be less than the $1000 face value. The reason is that buyers would rather purchase a T-bond with a 10 percent return for the same $1000 than buy your 8 percent bond.

Bear in mind that Treasury obligations are actively traded in the secondary market, so they are relatively liquid. If you must sell a Treasury obligation before maturity, you'll earn interest on it up to the day of sale. Also, some Treasury bonds contain call provisions, allowing the government to redeem the bond at any time within 5 years of the maturity date. And on the topic of these government obligations, what's right with America is a willingness to discuss what's wrong with America.

19

U.S. Savings Bonds— Safety First

Patriotism is not so much protecting the land of our fathers as preserving the land for our children.

When I was in public school, World War II was under way and the sale of war bonds was very popular. Every adult bought them. Children could purchase, in small amounts, freedom stamps (10 cents or 25 cents) that were then pasted into a "victory book." When this booklet was filled ($18.75), it was turned into the bank and exchanged for a savings bond with a face value at maturity of $25. Well, things have certainly changed. Years ago savings bonds were purchased to help our country finance and win World War II, but today they're purchased for completely different reasons. There are currently two types of U.S. savings bonds available—the Series EE bond and the Series HH bond. Let me explain both types and provide some insight as to their advantages and disadvantages as investment vehicles.

How Do EE Bonds Work?

The EE bond is a nonnegotiable security against the credit of the U.S. Treasury—nonnegotiable because once it is purchased it cannot be resold to anyone else but may be sold back only to the government at a fixed price. However, you are permitted to transfer the bonds to someone else by registering them in the person's name by filling out form PD3360. This form is available at any Federal Reserve district bank or by calling (304) 420-6112. Bear in mind that when you transfer the savings bonds, all accrued interest becomes taxable to you. You may also have to pay a gift tax if the bonds are worth more than $10,000. If, upon the death of an owner, there is a surviving co-owner or beneficiary named on the bonds, the bonds do not form a part of a decedent's estate for probate purposes. Subject to applicable estate or inheritance taxes, if any, they become the sole and absolute property of the survivor. Series EE bonds are sold at half their face value and are available in denominations of $50, $75, $100, $200, $500, $1000, $5000, and $10,000. Thus you can buy a savings bond for as little as $25, making it a practical choice for the investor with only a minimal amount of money to set aside.

The annual limit on the amount of Series EE Bonds an individual may buy is $15,000, issue price ($30,000, face amount). This limit applies to the amount of bonds that may be purchased in the name of any one person in any one calendar year; it has no effect on cumulative holdings. Purchasing bonds in co-ownership form effectively doubles the limit, if neither co-owner has purchased other bonds.

U.S. savings bonds are easy to buy. A new method for issuing savings bonds purchased over the counter is being implemented by the Treasury. The new system, referred to as the *regional delivery system* (RDS) consolidates responsibility for the inscription and issuance of these bonds with the Federal Reserve banks. Banks, savings and loans, and other financial institutions will continue to receive bond purchase applications and payments from their customers. However, instead of each financial institution issuing bonds directly, with RDS the purchase information will be forwarded to a Federal Reserve bank where the bonds will be issued and mailed to customers, usually within 2 or 3 weeks. If you like buying savings bonds as last-minute gifts, the banks will give you a gift certificate. You can also buy them on a regular basis through your employer's payroll-deduction plan. This is a very valuable service for those who find it hard to save unless forced to do so. With payroll deduction, the money to buy your bonds is taken out of your salary check before you get it, thus reducing the pain involved in saving and eliminating the temptation to spend the money rather than put it aside.

Years ago, U.S. savings bonds paid a notoriously low rate of interest. This now has changed. In 1982, the federal government realized that it was necessary to make savings bonds more competitive with higher-yielding investments such as money market funds. Therefore, the fixed interest schedule formerly used for savings bonds was changed to a variable rate. Each May 1 and November 1, the Treasury computes the average daily market yield on 5-year Treasury marketable securities during the preceding 6 months. The savings bond rate is set at 85 percent of the market average. At the end of 5 years, the average of the 10 semiannual rates, compounded semiannually, determines a bond's 5-year yield. If a bond is held for 6 years, 12 semiannual rates are averaged, and so on. Bonds held less than 5 years earn interest on a fixed graduated scale. There is also a minimum annual interest payout of 6 percent.

This new variable interest rate is a boon to investors because when market interest rates rise, the owner of U.S. savings bonds will now benefit from the higher yields rather than being locked into a low fixed rate as before. The 6 percent minimum rate will protect the investor in case interest rates take a dramatic plunge. For example, if the 5-year Treasury average is 12 percent, your EE bonds will pay 10.2 percent (85 percent of 12 percent). However, if the Treasury rate falls to 5½ percent, you'll still receive the minimum 6 percent on your EE bonds. To find out the latest interest rates on these bonds, call 1-800-US Bonds. Thus, U.S. savings bonds, while still not the highest-paying investment around, now offer a respectable yield along with their unmatched safety—safety not only for their guarantee of principal and interest, but also for their repayment should they be stolen, lost, or destroyed. If any of these situations occur, bonds can be replaced by notifying the Bureau of Public Debt, 200 Third Street, Parkersburg, West Virginia 26101-1328.

How Do You Redeem Savings Bonds?

Savings bonds are a relatively illiquid investment. You must hold onto your EE bonds for 5 years in order to receive the variable rate (or the 6 percent minimum). If you cash in your bonds before 5 years have passed, you will earn interest on a fixed, graduated scale that starts at 4.16 percent after the first 6 months and increases gradually every 6 months up to 5 years. Thereafter, the variable rate applies through the twelfth year of the life of the bonds, at which time they are mature. This means you are guaranteed that your money will at least double in 12 years, with the possibility of a greater return depending on interest rates. Earlier bonds, bought before November 1986, had a maturity date of just under 10 years (minimum rate was 7½ percent). Recently a revised timetable was established allowing you to hold the bonds past their maturity, still earning interest (see Table 19.1). This new ruling states that savings bonds issued before December 1965 have a 40-year maturity life, while bonds bought after that date have a 30-year maturity life. All previous maturities have now been extended to accompany the government's new timetable. Remember that taxes on the interest from these bonds are due when the bonds reach maturity whether or not you decide to cash them in at that time, so don't leave them lying around in your vault indefinitely.

The exact timing of your purchase and redemption of savings bonds can make a surprisingly large difference in the amount you will earn. Here's how it works. First, no matter what day of the month you buy your EE bonds, you'll be cred-

TABLE 19.1. EXTENDED FINAL MATURITY DATES FOR SERIES E/EE BONDS AND SAVINGS NOTES

Series	Date of issue	Date of maturity	Term of bond, years
Series E*	May 1941– November 1965	May 1981– November 2005	40
Series E†	December 1965–June 1980	December 1995–June 2010	30
Series EE	January 1980 and later	January 2010 and later	30
Savings notes	May 1967– October 1970	May 1997– October 2000	30

*All Series E bonds do not increase in value on the same basis. Maturity and yield have been revised several times; thus, older bonds have less redemption value than more current bonds.

†Series E bonds which have passed their final maturity dates have ceased to earn interest but may be redeemed at any time. All other Series E and EE bonds and savings notes will continue to earn interest until their final maturity. Series E bonds may be exchanged for Series HH bonds until 1 year after the Series E bond reaches final maturity; Series EE bonds are eligible for exchange 6 months after the date of issue; all savings notes are currently eligible for exchange.

ited with interest for the full month. This means that even if you buy the bond on the thirty-first of the month, you'll get credit for interest beginning on the first of that month. When you cash in your bond, other rules apply. If you hold the bond for 18 months or less, interest is credited on the first day of each month for the previous month. For example, if you cash in your bond on August 31, you'll receive interest through July 31 only. But if you can wait just one more day and cash in the bond on September 1, you'll be credited with interest for the month of August.

If you hold the bond for 19 months or more, interest is

credited every 6 months, starting from the month of purchase. For example, if you bought a bond 15 years ago during January, you would have to wait until July 1 to be sure of receiving interest for the full 6-month January-to-July period. If you cashed in the bond even 1 day too soon, you'd lose 6 months' interest. So take a close look at your calendar before you head to the bank to redeem your bonds. The following rule should be easy to understand: In whatever month you purchase a savings bond (the month is stamped on the bond), consider that month as the first month of a 6-month cycle and sell the bond in the seventh month.

You may receive information about maturity dates by writing to U.S. Savings Bonds Division, Department of the Treasury, Office of Public Affairs, Department CT, Washington, D.C. 20226; request form PD3600. While writing, ask for the following booklets: "Savings Bonds Questions and Answers Book" and "The Best Times to Redeem or Exchange Savings Bonds." For more specific information, tables of redemption values for savings bonds are published regularly and are available from the U.S. Government Printing Office, Washington, D.C. 20402. Banks can also provide information on redemption values to bond owners.

How Do Taxes Affect the Bonds?

The interest payout on U.S. savings bonds is tax-exempt at the state and local level but is subject to inheritance and estate taxes levied by states and localities. It is tax-deferred at the federal level. That is, the interest you receive is paid in one lump sum at the time of redemption and is fully taxable in that year. You can avoid a heavy tax liability by buying savings bonds in your child's name and treating each year's interest income as reportable as earned. Here's how it works. File a tax return for your youngster in the year you buy the bond. This shows the IRS that you intend to report the interest income from the bond annually rather than in total upon redemption. You can get yearly interest rates on tables published in the Treasury's PD3501 pamphlet. As long as the income generated from the bond is under $1000 (assuming no other income from other sources), it will be taxed at the child's lower tax rate if he or she is under age 14. After age 14, all income, regardless of amount, is taxable at the child's rate. But note that once the child elects to declare the EE income annually, he or she must do so with all future bonds purchased for 5 years. And bear in mind that the youngster is entitled to the standard deduction of $550 because a separate tax return (form 1040) has been filed in his or her name. If the bond interest is the major source of income, he or she will pay little or no tax on this income. Also, the parents will not lose their child's personal exemption that they are still permitted to take as a deduction on their own return.

If you intend to use this method to save on taxes, be sure to take two precautions: First, save a copy of your child's income tax form until you've redeemed the bonds. Second, don't put your name or anyone else's on the bond as co-owner. The instrument must be in the child's name only, so that the child is presumed to be the owner no matter who paid for the bond. This tax-saving technique is most appropriate for use with bonds that are intended for savings to benefit the child—a college tuition fund, for example.

What Role Do Bonds Play in Plans for College?

On January 1, 1990, a new education savings bond program began that permitted qualified taxpayers to exclude from their gross income all or a part of the interest earned on savings bonds bought after that date. This tax-free income (federal, state, and local) is permitted if the proceeds of the bond are used only for the child's college fees, which do not include room, board, or books.

To the middle-income investor, the tax-free status that these savings bonds might yield could become impressive. For example, if the payout on the bond should average 8 percent, this would actually have the effect of an 11.1 percent interest rate for the individual in the 28 percent tax bracket. And remember that these savings bonds are also exempt from state and local taxes, so the yield would be even higher than the 11.1 percent, depending upon the state in which you live.

It sounds great, but is it really? The conditions that must be met are quite numerous and will in essence disallow this tax loophole for most people. In order to get this tax-free income, the following conditions must prevail:

1. The child cannot own the bond. The bond must be bought and owned by the parents, who must be over 24 years of age. Grandparents cannot buy the bonds for their grandchildren.

2. If your "modified" adjusted gross income (your AGI plus the taxable portion of social security benefits, plus any deductible contributions you made toward your IRA) is more than $60,000 if you file jointly or $40,000 if you are single (this income level is considered at the time of redemption and not at the purchase date), the bonds will begin to lose their tax-free nature. A portion of the interest can be still considered tax-exempt over these levels, but couples whose income exceeds $90,000 or singles whose income exceeds $55,000 will not be able to get the tax-free advantage. These income limits will rise each year based on the inflation rate (rounded to the nearest multiple of $50), but you will not know what they will be until you finally redeem the bonds. The problem is obvious. You could invest money in these savings bonds for years and then find out when your child enters college that you fail to qualify because your income has outpaced inflation. Also, married individuals filing separately will not be allowed to use the program regardless of their income.

3. Your yearly expenses for college tuition must be more than what you receive in the same year from the bonds you redeem. For example, if you receive $8000 for the bonds,

$4000 of which is interest, and you spend $6000 in college costs, you will be allowed only $3000 as an exemption (75 percent of the $4000 interest). The 75 percent figure is used because only $6000 of the $8000 (that is, three-fourths, or 75 percent) has been used for acceptable college expenses. Therefore, it is important that you attempt to balance what you receive in bonds each year with your annual tuition costs.

4. You do not have to declare how you intend to use the money from the savings bonds when you purchase them, but you must be ready to show evidence that the money was used for educational purposes when you cash in the bonds.

5. The standard limitation of $30,000 face value or $15,000 purchase price (or $60,000 and $30,000 for husband and wife holding bonds as co-owners) in bonds per year applies to the education bond program as well as to all EE issues. However, there is no limit to the amount of bonds that can be accumulated for educational expenses over time.

For more information about savings bonds for college education write to the Office of Public Affairs, U.S. Savings Bond Division, Department CT, Washington, D.C. 20226.

How Do HH Bonds Work?

Up to this point, we've been discussing EE bonds only. The HH bonds are different in several ways. Unlike EE bonds, HH bonds pay interest on a semiannual basis. Therefore, the interest income is taxable as it is earned throughout the life of the bond. The HH bonds mature in 20 years, pay 6 percent interest annually, and are available in denominations of $500, $1000, $5000, and $10,000.

You can't buy HH bonds for cash, however. They can be acquired only in exchange for (1) EE bonds, (2) the older E bonds, or (3) savings notes ("freedom shares"), which were issued between 1967 and 1970. By making this transfer, the holder can continue to defer taxes. Therefore if your income is likely to drop during the 20 years (the life of HH bonds), you will benefit from this deferral. These changes can be made by any of the 12 Federal Reserve banks and their 24 branches, or by using form PD3253, which can be secured at any bank.

Any month after June is a good time to make the switch. For example, if you swap EE bonds for HH bonds during June 1991, the first payment of HH interest to you won't be made until January 1992. This means that you will not have to declare the income until 1993, when you file your 1992 return.

Why would anyone turn in their EE bonds to get HH bonds? It's a way of stretching out and so limiting the income tax liability that goes along with the lump-sum interest payout characteristic of EE bonds. The interest payable on your mature EE bonds isn't taxable at the time you exchange them for HH bonds. Instead, the amount of interest accumulated on the EE bonds is stamped on the face of the HH bonds. That amount is not taxable as current income until you cash in your HH bonds, which may not happen for quite a while— not until after retirement, for example, at which time your income and tax bracket could be lower. If you're planning on retiring fairly soon, it's a good idea to exchange your EE bonds for HH bonds rather than simply cashing them in. But don't hold them for the full 20-year period. At the low 6 percent payout, you are better off cashing them in (once you are retired) and investing the money in a higher-yielding instrument. If that money is placed in tax-free municipal bonds, you'll end up having to return less in taxes on profits. And on the topic of taxes, remember that any government big enough to give you everything you want is big enough to take everything you've got.

20
Zero Investment

Dig a well before you are thirsty.

The zero coupon bond is a unique financial tool which has become, over the years, an increasingly popular instrument for long-term investment. As you will see in the following pages, zero coupon bonds have some definite advantages over other types of long-term investments. They have become an excellent choice for individual retirement accounts (IRAs), 401(k) plans, Keogh and other pension funds, and most certainly for a child's college savings. They are therefore an ideal investment for those of you who are more concerned about "outcome" rather than "income."

How Does the Zero Coupon Bond Work?

Bonds are a debt obligation issued by a corporation or by an agency of the federal, state, or local government. When you buy a bond (usually at face value), you are buying a promise from the issuing institution to pay the amount of the face of the bond at maturity. However, unlike the traditional bonds mentioned above, "zeros" are sold at a price well below the face value. Thus, these bonds are appealing to the small investor because they can be bought far more cheaply than the ordinary debt obligations. The discount is usually from 50 to 75 percent. For example, a zero with a face value of $1000 (at 8 percent) may sell for just $456. You pay $456 today; at the time of maturity—usually in 10 years—you can redeem the bond for its full $1000 face value. The extra $544 paid on redemption is the accumulated 10 years' worth of interest on your $456 investment.

During the life of the zero, you clip no coupons and receive no interest payments (hence the name *zero coupon bonds*). The entire interest payout comes at once—upon redemption.

Table 20.1 shows the price you'd have to pay for a $1000 zero coupon bond based on various interest rates and maturity dates. Note that the amounts are rounded to the nearest dollar. Naturally, the longer the term of the bond and the higher the interest rate, the greater the discount at which the bond is sold.

If you're still in your twenties or thirties, you may purchase a big chunk of retirement money very cheaply by buying a long-term zero right now. For example, at a 10 percent interest rate, you may buy a zero redeemable at $1000 in 30 years for only $54! It's hard to imagine a better buy than that.

TABLE 20.1. ZERO COUPON BONDS

Interest rate, %	Maturity date and cost, years*					
	5	10	15	20	25	30
6	$744	$554	$412	$307	$228	$170
7	709	502	356	255	179	127
8	676	456	308	208	141	95
9	644	415	267	172	111	71
10	614	377	231	142	87	54
11	585	343	201	117	69	40
12	558	312	174	97	54	30

*Actual price may vary because of availability, fees, and other factors affecting bond prices.

What Advantages Do Zeros Offer as an Investment?

Zero coupon bonds offer several distinct advantages. Zeros have *call protection,* meaning that it is unlikely that they will be called in for early redemption by the issuing company if interest rates should fall. (There'd be no advantage to the corporation in prepaying the interest on zeros unless there were special call provisions in the agreement.) Be certain to find out whether the bond you wish to purchase is callable and, if so, ask about its *yield to call.* Yield to call means that you will be guaranteed a set return if the bond is called in early. Also, if interest rates in the market should fall, with a conventional bond the interest payments you receive would have to be reinvested at the lower existing rate. You avoid this when you purchase zero coupon bonds because the interest is reinvested at the fixed rate (which was higher than the prevailing rate) at which you purchased them.

Zeros also offer liquidity. If, for some reason you need to sell your bond before maturity, you can sell it on the so-called secondary market at the current rate. This may produce a gain or loss depending upon current interest rates at the time of the sale. For example, if interest rates are higher at the time you dispose of the bonds, you will take a loss. However, a lower interest rate will yield you a profit. And speaking about interest rates, another advantage of zeros is that you avoid the roller-coaster ups and downs of interest rates if the bond is kept to maturity. You are aware that the value of a bond will rise if interest rates fall and will drop in value if interest rates rise. Zero bonds are an exception because no matter how much their value may fluctuate and fall, at maturity the bond will be redeemed at its face value. This gives you the assurance of knowing exactly what you will receive at a certain time in the future.

Most important, zeros adapt themselves very well to a variety of personal financial plans. Because you know exactly how much money you'll be receiving for your investment and exactly when the payout will occur, you can make long-range plans based on your investment in zeros. Thus, they make an excellent choice for your IRA, if you still qualify, or Keogh plan investment, allowing you to accumulate tax-deferred interest at a fixed rate until retirement. This is because the annual earnings of the IRA or Keogh (known as *imputed interest*) are not subject to annual tax until they are withdrawn.

Are Zero Coupon Bonds a Good Investment Vehicle for Education?

Zero coupon bonds are also an excellent way of saving for your child's college tuition. That newborn baby is certainly a joy today but, financially, a major cost problem years from now. It has been estimated that the average cost of 4 years of college could be as high as $200,000 at private ivy league schools by the time that newborn reaches 18 years of age.

You can invest in zeros which will mature at the time your child is ready for school and, at the same time, greatly reduce or minimize the tax bite on the interest if you handle the transaction properly. Remember, under the Tax Reform Act (TRA), only the first $1000 of your child's unearned income will be taxed at his or her low rate, the first $500 being exempt (because of the standard deduction). This means that by reporting the interest each year on the child's return, you will get that exemption 18 times (assuming an 18-year bond). However, if the interest were to be reported in one lump sum only (as with some instruments), you would be able to use the $500 exemption only once. Also, by paying the tax each year, you do not have to concern yourself about having a lump-sum amount that is taxable come due just when you are about to pay for your child's college tuition.

And one more point on this topic. Make absolutely certain that the zeros mature when the child is past the age of 14, as all income will be subject to the child's lower rate. To avoid any tax to the child, consider the zero coupon municipal

bond (see page 159), after $1000 of annual interest income is
reached.

What Are the Disadvantages of the Zero Coupon Bond?

Zero coupon bonds do have some disadvantages. The degree
of risk is one. If the company issuing the bonds is no longer
solvent at the time of maturity, you may lose your entire investment. The possibility of default is a serious consideration
with bonds of every kind, but the problem is especially significant with zeros. This is because you receive all interest payments at once, upon maturity, whereas with other types of
bonds you receive interest on a regular basis throughout the
life of the bond.

A second disadvantage involves the markup that brokers
add to the wholesale price of the bonds. The cost to purchase
a zero is much higher (percentage-wise) compared with that
of an ordinary bond because of the broker's markup, which
is based on face value rather than cost. For example, a $30
commission on an ordinary $1000 (face value) bond is only 3
percent, but on the much smaller price of a zero (on a $300
zero it would be 10 percent) the same $30 commission would
be quite high. It is very difficult for an investor to determine
what the markup is on zero coupon bonds because the bonds
are sold "net." Brokerage houses buy them at wholesale and
resell them to the general public at retail prices. The markup,
which is used instead of a sales commission, will increase the
price of the zero and will reduce the price you get when you
sell.

The only way to know whether your broker is charging you
a fair price is to shop around. Call other brokerage houses to
see what the competition has to offer. Remember that the
larger the broker's markup, the more the bond will cost, leaving you with a smaller yield. Also, prices of zeros change every
day, so if you are seeking the best rate, do all your shopping
on the *same* day in order to compare fairly.

When comparing brokers, ask each of them the following questions:

1. How much will I have to invest in order to get the bond (zero) that I want?
2. How much will that investment be worth at maturity?
3. What is the effective yield to maturity?

The broker who can give you the lowest figure for question 1 and the highest figures for questions 2 and 3 will be getting you your money's worth. Just as a sidelight, those investors who got hurt in the market crashes of 1987 and 1989 felt that they are called a "broker" because after you use them you are.

A third disadvantage involves taxes. Although you receive no cash payments during the life of the zero coupon bond, you are taxed as if you do, because zero coupon bond interest must be reported to the IRS each year. After 18 years, a zero bought for $200 might grow to $1000 at maturity. To report the $800 interest, you do not take $\frac{1}{18}$ of it ($44 each year), but report the interest as it actually accrues. During the first year, a $200 investment earning 8 percent would produce approximately $16. In the second year your investment would not be $200 but $216 ($200 + $16), and $17.28 would be the interest that year. You do not have to personally compute this every year as you will receive a notice from the issuer or your broker informing you of the amount of interest to report to the IRS. The tax on this "invisible interest," also known as "phantom income," can be considered a major drawback of zero coupon bonds because you are forced to pay tax on income you haven't received and will not receive for many years. To avoid this problem, look into the zero coupon municipal bond.

What Is a Zero Coupon Municipal Bond?

A *zero coupon municipal bond* is a bond which performs the same as a zero coupon corporate bond but is issued by a state or local government agency, with the bond's maturities ranging from 7 to 30 years. Because it is a municipal bond, the interest you earn is exempt from all federal taxes and, in many cases, if the bond is issued within your state, from state and local taxes as well. The gains you receive at maturity are considered tax-free income which has accrued annually from the time of the issuance of the bonds.

Those attracted to zero coupon bonds should also consider one more alternative: zeros issued by the U.S. Treasury, the safest of the three types. These are sometimes called by other names, such as *stripped Treasuries,* a name given by brokerage houses which "strip" smaller investment units from large Treasury bonds for sale to investors.

The most valuable feature of the zero coupon bond is that it lets you know exactly how much money you'll have at a particular future date, which facilitates financial planning for the years to come. Tell your broker when you'd like your bonds to mature, and he or she can let you know when zeros that meet your needs are available. And on the topic of the future, many people worry a lot today about tomorrow because they didn't worry a little yesterday about today.

PART 2

Financial Planning for the Future

21

Planning Your Retirement—An Overview

Retirement takes all the fun out of Saturdays.

In the following chapters, various retirement plans are discussed. Whether you are employed by a corporation or a state or governmental agency, are self-employed, or are working part-time, some of the options explained in the following pages will affect your future financial plans.

How Do Lump-Sum Distributions Work?

Every day, for various reasons, people are receiving large lump-sum distributions representing the accumulated value of their pension plans. This may occur when you retire, or it may occur sooner if you become disabled, if you leave your present employer, or if the company decides to terminate your pension plan. In any case, when you receive such a lump-sum distribution, you face a problem: How do you minimize the taxes on this often sizable payment?

There are basically two solutions: (1) 5-year forward averaging for tax purposes and (2) an individual retirement account (IRA) rollover. Let's consider both these techniques.

What Is the 5-Year Forward Average Plan?

You may be acquainted with ordinary income averaging, which is a way of reducing your income taxes for a year in which your income is markedly higher than in previous years. Five-year forward averaging is slightly different in that it allows your lump-sum distribution to be taxed at a different, lower rate than your other income. Here's how it works.

When you use 5-year forward averaging, your lump-sum distribution is taxed as if you were receiving it in five equal annual payments. For each of the 5 years, you pay taxes on just one-fifth of the total distribution. Furthermore, the tax on each installment is computed as though the lump-sum distribution were your only source of income for the year, which is then added to your other income tax payments for the year. The tax is likely to be far less than it would be if it were computed as part of your entire year's income. Under the Tax Reform Act (TRA), if you were age 50 by January 1986, you can use 10 years instead of 5 years in computing forward averaging, if you use specific tax rate tables. On a $100,000 distribution, you would owe the IRS $15,943 with the 5-year forward average, $14,471 with the 10-year method, and $28,000 using no averaging.

In order for you to use either method, your distribution must come from a qualified plan in which you have been enrolled for at least 5 years, the sum must represent your entire interest in the plan, and you must be at least age 59½.

If you decide to forward average (either 5- or 10-year plan), the tax law requires you to the method on all other lump sums you receive in the same year from any other tax-deferred plan. In other words, you cannot forward average one lump sum and roll over others into an IRA.

What Is an IRA Rollover?

Another way to reduce the taxes on your lump-sum distribution is to roll it over—that is, reinvest it—in an IRA. This must be done within 60 days of receiving the distribution or you will lose the tax-shelter status otherwise conferred by the IRA. You don't have to pay any current income taxes on the distribution amount if you deposit it in an IRA, nor will you owe taxes on the income which accumulates in the account. The IRA funds become taxable only upon withdrawal, which may begin after you reach age 59½ and must begin by age 70½.

Which Method—5-Year Averaging or IRA Rollover—Is Better?

The answer to this question depends on your personal financial situation. If you plan to retire and liquidate your IRA in a short time—say 4 years or less, then the 5-year forward averaging method is likely to save you more money. This is because, once you begin withdrawing your IRA funds, the money is usually taxed at a higher rate than that called for under 5-year averaging.

Another consideration is the level of income you expect to enjoy after retirement. If you expect your income to decline sharply upon retirement, then an IRA rollover plan is probably your best choice. Chances are that, under those circumstances, the taxes you'll pay when withdrawing your IRA funds will be relatively low. On the other hand, if income from other sources will keep you in a fairly high tax bracket when you retire, then the 5-year forward averaging plan is best. Pay the low 5-year averaging rate and invest the distribution amount in an appropriate tax-saving instrument such as municipal bonds. As with most financial decisions, several factors must be taken into account, and only you can decide which is most important to you.

How Does Early Retirement Play a Role in the Various Plans?

There is a story of a beautiful bird who was powerful and free. It had magnificent colorful plumage of which it was very proud. One day the bird decided to pluck its feathers, one by one, in order to make a nest in which it could rest in comfort and security. Now it cannot fly.

Don't consider retiring until you are both financially and emotionally ready. Why? Because people have not been properly prepared for retirement in America. We spend a third of our lifetime preparing for a career, but almost no time in preparing for the period afterward. There are thousands of books and pamphlets on retirement, but most do not cover the most important consideration: the feeling of being retired. Today's unanswered question seems to be not so much what happens physically to people when they retire as what happens emotionally to them. The American public, the government, and the medical profession put more effort into helping folks reach old age than in helping them to enjoy it. Can you imagine filling 10 hours a day (3650 hours a year) in leisure? That huge amount of time hangs over every retired person like unspent capital.

The prevailing vision of the good life in this country may be a mirage. Generally speaking, America does not seem to like old people; and retired people—whether you accept it or not—are old people, which means at any age of retirement, whether it be 60 or 70. Older people are of interest mainly to doctors and hospitals, real estate brokers, and travel agents—not as people but as a source of income. As your ability to earn money decreases, so, too, does your stature as a person.

So be very careful when you decide at what age you will leave the work force. The decision to retire will be based on your financial status, and careful planning is mandatory. For example, people who are nearing retirement or have begun retirement with a fixed asset base may be concerned whether their money will last as long as it will be needed. If you are forced to dip into your principal in order to make ends meet, Table 21.1 may be of great help to you. It shows how long your money will last if you must draw from it at a rate faster than it is growing. As an illustration, suppose your assets are earning a 9 percent annual rate and you must withdraw 15 percent of your principal each year in order to live comfortably in retire-

TABLE 21.1. EARNINGS AND WITHDRAWALS

If principal is earning at this rate	And you are withdrawing at this rate										
	16%	15%	14%	13%	12%	11%	10%	9%	8%	7%	6%
12%	12	14	17	23							
11	11	13	15	18	24						
10	10	12	13	15	19	25					
9	10	11	12	14	16	20	27				
8	9	10	11	12	14	17	21	28			
7	9	9	10	11	13	15	18	22	31		
6	8	9	10	11	12	13	16	19	24	33	
5	8	8	9	10	11	12	14	17	20	26	37

Here's how many years your principal will last

ment. As shown in the table, your money should last approximately 11 years.

The following chapters should be of value to you in determining the various option plans for your retirement. And on the topic of retirement, before you decide to retire, take a week off and watch daytime TV.

22
The IRA

*You can plan for tomorrow today but you
can't plan for today tomorrow.*

The *individual retirement account (IRA)* is a method of investing
originally designed to help individuals not covered by company pension plans save for their retirement. On January 1,
1982, the law governing IRAs was changed to make them
available to anyone with earned income (wages, fees)
whether or not the individual was covered by a company pension plan. The law was changed again in January 1987 to limit
the amount deductible from your income tax (see page 169).

How Does the IRA Work?

First, some basic ground rules. Your IRA is a savings account
containing funds that can be invested in any of a number of
different financial instruments. (I'll offer some guidelines on
your options in a moment.) By law, you may contribute to
your IRA up to 100 percent of the first $2000 that you earn
each year. If a husband and wife are both working, they can
establish an IRA and contribute up to $2000 per year to each
account, for a family total of $4000. If one spouse does not
work, up to $2250 may be contributed, with a maximum of
$2000 in one account. Many advertisers are touting the fact
that a $2000 annual deposit into an IRA (at 10 percent) by a
25-year-old would be worth nearly $1 million ($973,704)

when the person reached age 65. Table 22.1 shows the value for different years and rate yields for a constant $2000 annual contribution. The figures are impressive.

But here is where the rules changed under the Tax Reform Act (TRA). If you or your spouse is considered an active participant in a qualified pension plan (even if you do not as yet have vested rights), you will have limits imposed on your IRA contribution. You can still contribute up to $2000 as long as your adjusted gross income (AGI) is not more than $25,000 (individual) or $40,000 (joint). If you are an individual filer earning between $25,000 and $35,000 or a joint filer earning between $40,000 and $50,000, your deductible amount of $2000 will be reduced by 20 percent of your income over $25,000 (individual) and $40,000 (joint). For example, a taxpayer (individual) earning $28,000 may deduct, for tax purposes, only $1400 of the $2000 contribution, that is, $2000 less $600 (20% × $3000, the excess over $25,000). Table 22.2

TABLE 22.1. VALUE OF PRINCIPAL FOR $2000 YEARLY IRA CONTRIBUTION

Year	Interest rate			
	6%	8%	10%	12%
1	$2,120	$2,160	$2,200	$2,240
5	11,951	12,672	13,431	14,230
10	27,943	31,291	35,062	39,309
15	49,345	58,649	69,900	83,507
20	77,985	98,846	126,005	161,397
25	116,313	157,909	216,364	298,668
30	167,603	244,692	361,887	540,585
35	236,242	372,204	596,254	966,927
40	328,095	599,562	973,704	1,718,285

TABLE 22.2. MAXIMUM IRA DEDUCTIONS FOR
MID-RANGE INCOMES

Individual	Joint	Maximum IRA deduction
$25,000	$40,000	$2000
26,000	41,000	1800
27,000	42,000	1600
28,000	43,000	1400
29,000	44,000	1200
30,000	45,000	1000
31,000	46,000	800
32,000	47,000	600
33,000	48,000	400
34,000	49,000	200
35,000	50,000	0

shows the maximum deduction you may take if your income
falls within the mid-range. As of this writing (1991), proposals
are being made to modify the exclusions for IRAs.

What Are the Tax Consequences of the IRA?

The money you contribute to your IRA is deducted from your
income for tax purposes, providing immediate tax benefits,
and is called a *deductible contribution*. Although individual
filers in a pension plan with incomes over $35,000 and joint
filers in a pension plan with incomes over $50,000 cannot
make deductible contributions, they still can make nondeductible contributions up to $2000, with the earnings from
that amount accumulating tax-free. These nondeductible
contributions can be withdrawn without penalty, but the in-

terest earned on them, if withdrawn, is subject to tax and a possible early withdrawal penalty if taken out before you reach age 59½. Under the TRA there is a special treatment for deductible and nondeductible withdrawals. The TRA requires that you combine all IRA monies (both deductible and nondeductible) and pay tax on a prorated portion withdrawn. For example, a taxpayer who has $10,000 in IRAs ($8000 in a deductible account and $2000 in a new, nondeductible one) must lump them together for computation of withdrawal. If the taxpayer takes out $2000, only 20 percent, or $400, would be considered to come originally from the nondeductible IRA contribution. The balance of $1600 would be considered from the deductible IRA and would be subject to tax.

What Are the Rules for IRA Distributions?

Since the IRA was created specifically to make it easier for working people to save for their retirement, there are built-in restrictions on your access to IRA funds. You can begin withdrawing your IRA money without penalty after reaching age 59½. If you must withdraw the money before that time, you will have to pay an extra 10 percent tax on the amount you withdraw as a penalty, unless you're disabled.

One point must be noted at this time. New rules allow an individual to withdraw funds from an IRA without penalty (before age 59½) as long as the individual makes equal withdrawals each year in predetermined amounts. This method of withdrawal (called *annuitizing*) is designed to deplete the amount of money in the IRA over the life expectancy of the person. To those individuals who wish to retire in their fifties, this withdrawal option is of great benefit because it allows them to supplement their income until their social security benefits begin at age 62. Also, parents can now tap their IRAs before age 59½ to help pay the high costs of education for their children. What is important is that the IRA funds are able to be withdrawn under the annuity plan for any purpose without any justification needed. Even if the person was not able or eligible for the $2000 contribution, proceeds from pension plans, for example, can be rolled over into the IRA and the withdrawal plan option can be utilized for these funds. Also, and most important, once the yearly withdrawals begin, they must continue at the same rate for at least 5 years. A change after that period of time is permitted as long as the person is over 59½. Therefore, a 55-year-old would be able to (1) stop making annual withdrawals, (2) change the amount of withdrawal, or (3) withdraw the entire balance at age 60. Just remember that by tapping the IRA funds, you are reducing the basic financial structure for your retirement years and also your ability to have your money grow through tax-deferred savings.

The penalty for early withdrawal deters many young people from opening IRAs. When you're 25 years old, 59½ may seem an eternity away, and more than 20 years may seem like an impossibly long time to tie up your money. However, the effects of the penalty aren't nearly as severe as you might think. Because of the tax benefits derived both at the time of the contribution and during the accumulation of tax-free interest, IRA accounts become profitable fairly quickly even when the penalty for early withdrawal is taken into account. With 5 or 6 years of compounding, your income will more than compensate for the withdrawal penalty. After that time, even if you incur the 10 percent penalty, you will have increased your money faster than otherwise possible because of the tax benefits. Therefore, don't let the early withdrawal penalty discourage you unduly. An IRA is still a highly beneficial investment to have.

You *must* begin withdrawing your IRA funds by age 70½. As the funds are withdrawn, they are taxable as regular income for that year. However, your income will probably be lower after you retire, and the rate at which you'll be taxed will be lower as well.

You can withdraw the money in a lump sum or in installments, as you wish. If you choose the installment method, you must follow a schedule based on your life expectancy as determined by standard actuarial tables. For example, a 70-year-old man has a life expectancy of 12 years; a 70-year-old woman, 15 years. Therefore, the 70-year-old man who wishes to begin withdrawing his IRA funds must withdraw one-twelfth of the total amount in his account in the year, while the woman must withdraw one-fifteenth of her total. The penalty for failing to follow this schedule is stiff: For every dollar you fail to withdraw on schedule, you lose 50 cents.

There are two notable variations on this withdrawal scheme. In 1985, the law was modified to allow you to refigure your life expectancy each year. Since the older you get, the greater your expected age of demise becomes, annually refiguring your life expectancy will allow you to reduce the fraction that must be withdrawn from your IRA each year.

A second change in the law allows you to extend your IRA withdrawal period to cover the combined life expectancy of you and your spouse. This figure will usually be higher than the life expectancy of either husband or wife. For example, as stated previously, a 70-year-old man is expected to live 12 years, a 70-year-old woman, 15 years. However, one or the other can be expected to survive for 18 years. Therefore, the 70-year-old couple can use the 18-year life expectancy figure as the basis of their withdrawals if they wish—and they can recalculate their combined life expectancy each year as well.

What Happens If You Die before You Use Your IRA Funds?

There are several possibilities. When you start an IRA, you designate a beneficiary. When you die, your beneficiary may choose any of the following options:

1. Your beneficiary can withdraw IRA funds as a lump sum. The entire amount would be taxable during that year.

2. Your beneficiary can withdraw the IRA funds over a period of 5 years. During each of those years, the amount withdrawn that year is taxable.

3. Your beneficiary can withdraw the IRA funds and use them to purchase an annuity. The money would be taxable only at the time annuity benefits are paid based on a distribution of annual amounts over the beneficiary's life expectancy.

4. Your beneficiary (only a surviving spouse) can convert the IRA into his or her own account. The new owner will have all the rights and obligations you had.

What Investment Options Are Available for an IRA?

When you invest in an IRA, the law requires that a trustee be named to administer the account. The trustee must file reports with you and with the federal government. Typical IRA trustees include commercial and savings banks, savings and loan institutions, brokerage houses, insurance companies, and other types of investment firms.

As for the type of investment, any of a wide range of choices may be suitable for your IRA, depending on your age and financial status and the degree of risk you wish to take. The only restrictions on IRA investments are these: You may not invest your IRA funds in collectibles, such as postage stamps, coins (except certain U.S. gold and silver coins), antiques, or art; you may not invest your IRA funds in life insurance contracts; and you may not make an investment in which you have a direct interest, as, for example, if you were to buy a home with IRA funds and then rent it from the IRA account.

Here are some of the most popular investment choices for IRA accounts:

Certificates of deposit: An IRA bank account usually takes the form of a certificate of deposit with a minimum term of 18 months. Rates may be fixed in advance or variable. If rates are variable, find out just how the rate is set and how often it is adjusted—weekly, monthly, or whatever. In general, the most conservative investment strategy is to invest for the shortest available term.

Stocks and bonds: If you wish, you can deposit your IRA money with a stockbroker, who will act as your trustee. However, you direct the account yourself: You make your own investment decisions and you can buy and sell stocks and bonds, moving your funds from one investment to another, without incurring any taxes on the money.

Mutual funds: You can deposit your IRA money in a mutual fund, and so invest not in a few self-selected stocks but in a managed portfolio of many issues put together by a brokerage firm. You may wish to choose a broker who offers a "family of funds" of different types among which you are free to switch your investment from time to time without charge or penalty. Also, remember that there's no need to invest in any of the special tax-exempt mutual funds; your IRA investment is already sheltered from all levels of taxation. Stick to funds which are normally taxable; these usually offer a higher rate of return. Also, look into zero coupon bonds (see Chapter 20) for funding your IRA.

How Should You Choose among These Investment Options?

One prime consideration should be how well you have otherwise provided for your retirement. If your IRA is your sole retirement plan, you should invest conservatively; if you have substantial savings outside of the IRA, income which you expect to continue after retirement, or a secure company pension plan, you can afford a bit more risk. Your age is another important factor. Here are some guidelines to use depending on your present age:

Age 20 to 40: When you are young, growth should be your primary goal; a relatively high degree of risk is tolerable. Suggestion: Invest your IRA in a diversified portfolio of common stocks or in a mutual fund managed for growth of assets, not income.

Age 40 to 50: Stocks are still an attractive choice. However, if you expect to begin withdrawing your IRA funds when you reach age 59½, redirect some of your funds from growth stocks into current income-generating investments.

Age 50 to 60: At this point, growth is less important, risk less acceptable. Move your investments out of stocks and into bonds, in order to minimize risk and increase your current flow of income.

Age 60 and over: By now, all your IRA funds should be in income-producing investments with maturities of 5 years and less. This will provide safety and maximum current interest.

Is the IRA Transferable to Other Investments?

Once your IRA is in operation, you can move your money from one account to another in either of two ways—*direct transfer* or *rollover.* With direct transfer, the institution holding your IRA transfers it, at your request, directly to the new account, either at the same institution or elsewhere. You may move your IRA funds by direct transfer as many times as you like in order to take advantage of a changing investment situation without incurring any tax penalty. The rollover method may be used only once a year. It involves your taking possession of the IRA funds for up to 60 days. By the end of that time, you must have reinvested the funds in another IRA; otherwise, you will have to pay taxes on the amount held, along with any applicable penalties.

The IRA is certainly a plan to look into for your retirement, as it can become an excellent vehicle for future income. And on the topic of retirement plans, remember to plan for the future now because that is where you will be spending the rest of your life.

23

The 401(k) Plan

In two days, tomorrow will be yesterday.

An increasingly popular way of saving for retirement is the *401(k) plan,* named after the tax law provision that makes it possible. The 401(k) is known as the *deferred salary reduction plan* and allows an employee to set aside part of his or her salary into a tax-sheltered account that grows tax-free until after retirement. Don't confuse the 401(k) with a 403(b). A 403(b) is a retirement plan designed for employees of nonprofit organizations (schools, hospitals, etc.), whereas the 401(k) is for employees of private, for-profit businesses. Salary deductions for a 401(b) are treated in the same manner as the funds in the 401(k) account, which is excluded from your taxable income, while the interest earned compounds tax-deferred until you withdraw the funds.

How Does the 401(k) Differ from an Ordinary IRA?

Since you don't have to pay current income tax on the money you deposit in your 401(k) account, the plan is something like an individual retirement account. However, unlike an IRA, a 401(k) plan must be set up by your employer. And most employers who establish 401(k) plans make matching contributions on behalf of their employees—a wonderful benefit for you, if you're on the receiving end!

The 401(k) account differs from an IRA in other ways, too. Whereas the limit on contributions to an IRA is $2000 per year, you and your employer can make a combined investment contribution of up to $9500 per year or 25 percent of your salary (whichever is less) into your 401(k) account. With an IRA, you indicate the size of your contribution as a deduction on your federal income tax return. With a 401(k), this is not necessary. Your contribution is deducted from the income reported on your W-2 form, and therefore is automatically excluded from federal and state income taxes.

How Does the 401(k) Work?

Many 401(k) plans provide for employee contributions of 6 to 10 percent of salary, with equal amounts contributed by the employer. An employee earning $32,000 annually who participated in a 401(k) plan allowing an 8 percent salary deferral ($2560) would receive (and pay income tax on) only $29,440 in salary payments; the rest would be set aside until retirement. However, the full $32,000 would be subject to social security tax.

At the time the 401(k) plan is established by the employer, a specific investment program is set up. The employer usually chooses an investment firm to manage the accounts, and a range of possible investment options is offered. These choices are usually more restricted than they would be with an IRA. Whereas almost any investment vehicle is permissible with an IRA, only a handful of options are allowed with a 401(k): a fixed-interest annuity, a mutual fund investing in stocks, a money market fund, and, perhaps, stock in the company itself. You can opt to put all your contributions into one or another investment vehicle, or you can split your contributions among two or more choices.

What about Withdrawal from a 401(k)?

If you leave the company, you can withdraw your 401(k) savings and, if you like, you can keep the money. However, it becomes subject to income taxes during that year. You can avoid this by rolling the money over into an IRA. You are also eligible to withdraw your 401(k) money at any time without having to pay a penalty if you suffer a financial hardship.

Once you reach the age of 59½, the money in your 401(k) account is yours to do with as you please. Of course, it is taxable when you withdraw it. However, your income will probably be lower after you retire, and so might your tax bracket. And the 401(k) account has another major advantage over the IRA when withdrawal time comes. If you withdraw your IRA funds in a lump sum, you must suffer a big tax bite during that year. However, if you withdraw your 401(k) funds in a lump sum, you can use 5-year forward averaging to spread out and reduce the tax payments. This means that the withdrawal is taxed as if you'd received only one-fifth of the money each year for a period of 5 years. You may use 10-year forward averaging if you were born before 1936, but the tax rate table is different.

As you can see, the 401(k) plan is a very attractive investment option for employees, especially since the usual employer matching-contribution program in effect doubles your annual savings at no cost to you. More and more employers are offering 401(k) plans as part of their fringe benefit packages and to supplement existing pension plans. In some regions, over half of all companies are currently offering or plan to offer 401(k) plans. If your employer is among those making this investment option available, take advantage of it. And if you can afford to contribute to both a 401(k) account and an IRA, do that, too. You'll benefit right now as well as when you retire. And on the topic of retirement, the saddest part of growing older is looking back and realizing that every day was the tomorrow you were waiting for.

24

The Simplified Employee Pension (SEP)

Work is the recreation of the retired.

For a small business (proprietorship, partnership, corporation) the *simplified employee pension,* or *SEP,* is an excellent method for pension plans as it can help business owners, including those self-employed, to achieve financial security for their retirement. It was authorized in 1978 by Congress to give small businesses (even self-employed workers without employees) a program of current tax deduction and future pension benefits.

How Does the SEP Work?

The business sets up an IRA for each employee and contributes, each year, as much as $30,000 or 15 percent (13.043 percent for self-employed) of earnings. These contributions are tax-deductible to the company. Employees may decide how to contribute the funds to their IRAs and can take the IRAs with them when they leave the firm. There is no complex administration, and the start-up and maintenance costs are slight. One of the major features of the SEP is the extra time allowed to initiate it. Many people look for last-minute tax deductions before the April 15 deadline. You can set up a SEP 3½ months into the next year as compared with the Keogh plan, which requires completion by the last day of the year.

What Should You Know about the SEP?

1. The contributions made by the company to the SEP are tax-deductible to the company and are not considered taxable income of the employee. These monies accumulate in the employee's SEP/IRA on a tax-deferred basis.

2. No start-up or annual filing costs are required to be sent to the Department of Labor. As its name implies, it is a simple plan to administer. The paperwork usually amounts to no more than filling out once a model plan (5305-SEP). Unless changes are made in the plan, you do not have to file annually as you do with a Keogh.

3. All amounts from the SEP are considered ordinary income, with distribution of monies beginning no later than by age 70½. Any withdrawal prior to age 59½ may be subject to a 10 percent penalty.

4. All eligible employees must be included in the plan. Eligibility is based on the employee (1) being 21 years of age or older, (2) earning at least $327 per year, and (3) having worked for the business in 3 of the last 5 years.

5. The same percentage that the employer receives must be applied to each employee, including yourself.

6. Lump-sum distributions from the SEP do not qualify for special income averaging. Keogh plans (see the next chapter) allow this.

7. Unlike conventional company pension plans where the employees usually have to wait a number of years before they have access to their contributions, the SEP allows employees immediate right to any contributions the employer makes for their benefit.

Has the Tax Reform Act Changed the SEP?

Under the TRA, a type of SEP, known as *cash or deferred arrangement* (CODA), was created that permits each employee to make voluntary contributions (elective deferrals) to his or her own account. This contribution (20 percent of the employee's salary up to a maximum of $7979 per year) is considered to be a pretax contribution and therefore is not counted for federal income tax purposes. However, the amount will count as a deduction for social security. The total of the employer and employee contributions cannot exceed the lesser of $30,000 or 15 percent of total compensation.

SEPs were created to develop retirement plans for small businesses and their employees as well as for self-employed individuals who have no employees. The plan is an attractive way to save for those future retirement years while saving currently on taxes. And on the topic of retirement, the person who can't figure out what to do with a Sunday afternoon is often the one who can't wait to retire.

25

The Keogh Plan

Judge each day not by the harvest you reap,
but by the seeds you plant.

The Keogh plan is a form of pension plan designed for the self-employed individual whether the work is full- or part-time. In other words, you can work for an employer full-time, but if you have any income from self-employment, part of that self-employment income can be contributed to your own Keogh plan.

How Does the Keogh Plan Work?

A Keogh plan account is similar to an IRA in several ways. Your annual contribution to a Keogh account reduces your taxable income, and the sums in your account grow tax-free until you withdraw your investment after reaching the age of 59½; the upper limit on withdrawal is age 70½. At that time, the sums you withdraw are treated as ordinary taxable income. However, your income will probably be lower after retirement, so that the size of your tax bite will be smaller. Early withdrawals prior to age 59½ carry a 10 percent penalty. Therefore, as with an IRA, you should invest in a Keogh account only sums you don't expect to need until retirement. Liquidity is not one of the characteristics of a Keogh account.

What Are the Differences between the Keogh and the IRA?

As you will see subsequently, not everyone is eligible for a Keogh account. While the maximum amount you may contribute to an IRA in any year is $2000, you may invest up to a maximum of $30,000 or 25 percent of your earned income, whichever is less, in a Keogh account under the "money purchase" plan. This plan requires a fixed percentage of your income each year. If you have a "profit-sharing" Keogh, which allows varying contributions each year, the tax-deductible limit on contributions is 13.043 percent of your self-employment earnings, up to a maximum of $30,000.

Withdrawals from the two types of accounts are also handled differently. With both an IRA and a Keogh account, you can withdraw the money either in a lump sum upon retirement or in installments. However, if you withdraw your Keogh investment in a lump sum, you can take advantage of the 5-year forward averaging rule, which allows you to compute your taxable income as if the withdrawal had been spread out over a 5-year period. A 10-year forward averaging period is also available, subject to certain conditions. Thus the Keogh plan can produce significantly greater income tax savings at withdrawal time than the IRA.

How Do You Qualify for a Keogh Plan?

To qualify for a Keogh account, you must be self-employed as the sole proprietor of a business, an unincorporated professional, or a partner in any unincorporated partnership. In addition, if your business has any employees, you are required to include in the plan all those who have worked for you longer than 3 years. You must contribute to their retirement funds the same percentage of their salary that you are contributing to your own. (Naturally, the employer's share of the Keogh investment for employees is treated as a deductible business expense.) The Keogh funds may be invested in almost any kind of instrument favored by the employer, including a certificate of deposit, stocks and bonds, a money market fund, or an insurance account. Collectibles are virtually the only common type of investment not allowed. The employer may choose to manage the Keogh personally or may invest the money in an annuity contract purchased from an insurance company or a mutual fund managed by a broker.

Ever since their introduction, Keoghs have been among the most popular pension plans. In 1984, the contribution limits were raised from $15,000 or 15 percent of earned income to the present $30,000 or 25 percent. This change has only increased the attractiveness of the Keogh plan. If you're eligible for a Keogh plan account, you should certainly give it serious consideration as an investment option. It is a kind of super IRA which allows the self-employed professional or business proprietor to reduce his or her current taxable income while saving a substantial sum toward retirement. And on the topic of aging, as we get older, everything hurts, and what doesn't hurt, doesn't work.

26
Social Security

*I don't mind being a senior citizen, I just
don't look forward to graduation.*

People often overlook their social security benefits when calculating their projected retirement income. Financial planning is a system that must encompass all phases of investments, so know the rules of social security because for many
of us, it has become our most costly investment.

How Do Social Security Payments Work under the Tax Law?

Under the provisions of the 1984 Tax Reform Act, a formula
is used to determine the degree to which social security benefits are subject to income tax. This formula sets a "threshold
income" below which benefits are not taxed. The threshold is
$25,000 for single individuals and $32,000 for a married couple filing a joint return. Those whose income exceeds the
threshold amount may be subject to income tax on up to one-
half of their social security benefits.

To determine whether you exceed the threshold, you must
first compute what's called your *modified adjusted gross income.*
This consists of your adjusted gross income plus any otherwise tax-free interest income. For example, income derived
from tax-free municipal bonds must be included in this calculation. To this sum, add one-half of your social security bene-

fits and compare this total with the threshold figure. If it exceeds the threshold, your social security benefits are partially subject to taxation. The amount of taxable benefits is either half the amount by which you exceed the threshold or half of your social security benefits, whichever is less.

If you're confused, don't worry, for the following example will clarify the computation. Mr. and Mrs. Mohonk file a joint tax return. They have an adjusted gross income of $26,000, interest income which is exempt from federal income tax in the amount of $4000, and social security benefits of $10,000. Here's how they figure their taxable benefits:

$26,000	Adjusted gross income
+ 4,000	Tax-free income
30,000	Modified adjusted gross income
+ 5,000	Half of social security benefits
$35,000	

Now the Mohonks compare this $35,000 figure with their threshold figure of $32,000; there is an excess of $3000. Therefore, their social security benefits are taxable in the amount of either half the excess ($1500) or half their total benefits ($5000). Since the excess of $1500 is smaller than half of the Mohonks' social security benefits, $1500 is the amount of their benefits that is subject to tax.

For comparison's sake, let's change the example slightly. Suppose the Mohonks' tax-free interest income was $16,000 rather than $4000. Their computation would now be as follows:

$26,000	Adjusted gross income
+ 16,000	Tax-free interest income
42,000	Modified adjusted gross income
+ 5,000	Half of social security benefits
$47,000	

This amount ($47,000) exceeds the threshold by $15,000. Half the excess is $7500; half of the Mohonks' social security benefits is $5000. Since the latter figure is the smaller of the two, $5000 is the amount of the Mohonks' taxable benefits.

As you can see, this law adversely affects retirees with a high income, whether from tax-free or taxable sources. Those in the 28 to 31 percent tax bracket could lose up to 16 percent of their social security benefits in taxes.

An important additional point: The threshold for married couples filing jointly is $32,000, as noted above. However, the threshold for married couples filing separately is zero. This has been set in order to prevent married couples from escaping all taxation of social security benefits by filing separately, shifting all taxable income to one partner and all social security benefits to the other. Therefore, no matter what you may have heard, you will not benefit by filing separate returns instead of a joint return.

What Can You Do to Offset This Law?

If you're presently nearing retirement and have to choose whether to receive a lump-sum pension distribution this year or regular annuity payments in future years, take the lump-sum payment right now. The reason is simple. The lump-sum payment will not be subject to the social security benefits calculation this year, since you haven't retired yet. And it will qualify for a lower tax rate under the forward averaging plan. By contrast, if you choose the annuity payout, you may find that the payments after retirement will push your income to the threshold level, thereby making your retirement benefits subject to tax.

Another tax-saving tactic is to make a gift of tax-free investment instruments to your children. Municipal bonds are an example of instruments that can be used for this purpose. Your children, in turn, can return the interest payments to you in the form of a gift, which is not included in the social security computation. Of course, your children will then own the bonds. You must decide whether this is a reasonable option for yourself.

What Happens if You Want to Retire before Age 65?

Many individuals have asked me what I think about retiring before age 65. I have always felt that *it is better to retire too early than too late.* However, you have to understand the social security payout implications.

Consider retirement not as the goal of reaching retirement age, but as entering a retirement zone. At the center of this zone is the standard retirement age, which is 65 (if you were born before 1938) and 65 plus (up to a maximum of 67) if you were born after that date. At that center point you will be entitled to receive 100 percent of your primary insurance amount (PIA) as it is computed from your record earnings. On the low side of the retirement zone is age 62, which will provide you with early retirement benefits between 70 percent and 80 percent of your PIA. It is 80 percent if your full retirement age is 65 and 70 percent if your full retirement age is 67. If you decide to work past age 65, you move to the other side of the zone, known as the *high end.* At this point you will receive a higher monthly social security benefit (more than 100 percent) when you do finally retire. The amount will range from a 3.5 percent increase to an 8 percent increase depending on your date of birth. At age 70, you will have reached the highest end of the retirement zone, and will not receive any further increase in benefits. However, you do not have to retire to collect your full social security check because you are entitled, at this age, to full benefits, no matter how much you earn.

Also, as far as social security benefits are concerned, it makes no difference what time of the year you retire. Most people in fact retire toward the end of a calendar year simply as a matter of convenience and personal preference. However, the social security law permits you to retire at any time during the year without forfeiting any benefits; payments start any month you choose, provided you meet all the conditions of eligibility. When you've set your retirement date, plan on applying for social security benefits about 3 months earlier. This leaves plenty of time to process your claim and handle any questions or problems that may arise.

How Do You Know You Are Getting Accurate Social Security Benefits?

It would be unthinkable for a person to let years go by without balancing a checkbook; yet that same individual will usually wait until age 65 before making certain that his or her social security account has been accurately credited. By then, if there are errors, it may be too late. However, there is a way to remedy this situation while you are presently employed. Contact your social security office and ask for the free "Request for Earnings and Benefit Estimate" statement, which will verify your earnings record to date. Merely save your W-2s and compare the figures. Forty quarters of coverage will entitle you to receive full social security benefits at retirement. By periodically examining your social security account (every 3 years), you will be assured that the income paid from your account will represent all that you have earned.

Are There Any Penalties if You Work Part-time after You Retire?

Retirees who go back to work are subject to a most unpopular law known as the Retirement Earnings Test. This rule penalizes those who reenter the work force after they begin to collect social security. Congress, however, is already committed to taking one small step toward reducing the penalties on the working elderly. It has raised the limitations on earnings of those between the ages of 65 and 69 to $9720 in 1991 and cut the penalty on earnings over this ceiling to 33 percent. Between the ages of 62 and 64, the dollar amount is lowered to $7080, and the penalty increased to 50 percent. Once you reach age 70, you can collect full benefits, regardless of the amount of your earnings.

When social security was first set up during the Depression, one purpose was to push older workers out of the labor force to make room for unemployed younger people. That may not be desirable in the 1990s. And it may not be affordable after that. A move is under way in Congress to abolish completely the earnings penalty on seniors who are 65 or older. A single bill can't solve the complex problems of social security or create a happy balance among generational interests. However, it will begin to free people financially to experiment with new solutions and to lead more productive lives after age 65.

What Are the Family Benefits of a Social Security Plan?

The social security tax you and your employer pay places you and your family in line for collecting more than just retirement benefits. You may also collect Medicare and disability income. If you become disabled, you get benefits at any age (assuming you have enough quarters of coverage). In order to qualify for disability benefits, you must have earned 20 credits of coverage during the 10-year period ending with the calendar quarter you became disabled. However, if your disability is blindness or if you become disabled before reaching age 31, more lenient rules apply.

Your family members may also be entitled to payments based on your work history. For example, there are spousal benefits. Your spouse is entitled to retirement or disability benefits based on your earnings record. To qualify, a spouse must be at least 62 years old or care for a child under 16 who is also entitled to benefits. The spouse must have been married to you for at least 1 year or be the parent of your child.

In general, your spouse gets monthly checks equal to 50 percent of your retirement benefits, if that is more than he or she would get based on his or her own earnings record. Spousal benefits are also reduced if your wages exceed the earnings limit.

How Does Divorce Affect Spousal Benefits?

It has been said that divorce is the result when the bond of matrimony no longer bears interest. A divorced or surviving divorced spouse of a retired, disabled, or deceased worker can be eligible for spousal benefits and is treated as if the marriage had not been dissolved.

To qualify, the divorced spouse must have been married to the worker for at least 10 years. A divorced spouse is not entitled to collect benefits prior to age 62, even if he or she is caring for a child who is entitled to benefits. Benefits will not be reduced on account of the former spouse's having earnings in excess of the earnings limit, but they will be reduced if the divorcee-recipient's own earnings exceed the limit. Note that generally a divorced spouse's benefits end upon remarriage. However, divorced widow(er)s who are eligible for benefits do not lose them if they remarry after age 60 (50 for the disabled divorcees).

How Does the Death of the Insured Affect Social Security Payments?

A widow(er) or surviving divorced spouse can start collecting benefits at age 60 (50 if disabled). At age 60, a widow(er) will receive 71.5 percent of the amount the deceased spouse would have received at age 65, but if the surviving spouse waits until age 65, he or she will receive 100 percent of that amount. If death occurs while the insured is already collecting benefits, the spouse receives 100 percent of what the insured was collecting.

How Are Children Affected by Social Security?

A child (either natural or adopted) may be entitled to benefits upon the death of a parent. To qualify, the child must have been a dependent and (1) be unmarried and either under age 18, or if a full-time high school student, under age 19, or (2) regardless of age, be disabled before age 22. The child then would receive a monthly benefit equal to 50 percent of the amount you would get at age 65.

Bear in mind that there is a maximum on family benefits. The benefit percentages for family members are the maximum each relative can collect. When more than one family member is collecting benefits based on the insured's earnings record, the actual size of their benefit checks is likely to be smaller. Why? The social security law places a dollar cap on the total monthly benefits that are paid to a family based on the earnings of one family member.

Thus, you can see that in order to plan for retirement, all areas of income, whether actual or potential, must be considered. And on the topic of planning for retirement, remember that the time to fix the roof is when the sun is shining.

27
Will It?

The only real thing of value we can give our children is what we are, not what we have.

This final chapter is essential because of all the possible threats to your family's assets (inflation, downturn in the market, etc.) only one is definite, and that is your death. I have discussed in previous chapters, topics ranging from financial planning for young children through financial planning for retirement. Now this chapter completes the life cycle.

By law you have the right to own property, to use it as you wish during your lifetime, and to determine who shall receive it after you die. Everyone makes use of the first two rights, but many fail to exercise the third right by neglecting to write a will. Many people do not have a will, which is a shame because without one you lose control of your estate. This loss applies not only to what happens to what you own but also to who should receive the property after you die. Writing a will is a way of taking care of the people you love.

What Is a Will?

A *will* is simply a set of instructions as to what should be done with your property after you die. The *testator* (the person whose will it is) and the lawyer will both make important decisions today about events that will take place in the future and affect other people's lives. A will names your heirs, assigns specific shares of your property to each one, and describes any particular conditions under which the distribution should occur. If you fail to prepare a properly executed will, several unpleasant consequences may follow: Your property may not be distributed as you had hoped it would be, your heirs may suffer a greater tax burden and higher administrative costs, and your family and friends may be subject to needless worry and squabbling. Preparing a will is an essential part of meeting your financial responsibilities.

Who Carries Out the Instructions in a Will?

The instructions you leave in your will are to be carried out by a person you designate as the *executor*. If no one is named in the will as executor, the court will appoint an administrator. The job of executor is an important, sometimes burdensome, one, and it may include any or all of the following duties:

1. The executor must obtain a copy of the will and submit it to probate—that is, request court approval of its validity.

2. The executor may be required to publish a notice of death for a specified period of time.

3. The executor must inventory, appraise, and safeguard all assets of the estate.

4. The executor must open a checking account on behalf of the estate and maintain complete records of all transactions.

5. The executor must apply for all appropriate death benefits, including those available through life insurance, social security, pension plans, the Veterans Administration, labor unions, and fraternal organizations.

6. The executor must pay all outstanding debts of the deceased.

7. The executor must file and pay local, state, and federal income taxes, as well as estate taxes.

8. The executor must distribute all remaining assets according to the terms of the will.

9. Finally, the executor may be required to submit a final accounting to the court.

As you see, it's necessary to choose wisely when naming an executor, so it's best to make certain that the person you have in mind is willing to undertake the job and understand what it entails.

How Do You Begin to Draw Up a Will?

Before you consider who should receive your possessions at death, you must have some idea of what you own. Start by listing all your assets with their real or estimated value. The total is your gross estate. Because state and federal estate taxes can cut into your gross estate, it's important to know the exact value of your assets. If your taxable estate (equal to your gross estate less debts and expenses) exceeds $600,000, your survivors will face federal estate taxes—which can be steep. No federal tax is due, however, on the first $600,000 of value due (the unified tax credit). It should also be noted that no federal estate tax is due on assets left to your spouse or to a charity. The law varies from state to state on the estate tax that should be due.

Because personal and family circumstances change, you should review your will at least once every 5 years to make certain that it still reflects your current wishes and needs. You should change your will when any of the following events occur:

If you marry, separate, or divorce

If your beneficiary or executor dies

If you move to another state

If federal, state, or estate laws change

If family circumstances change

If financial matters change

If you change your mind

If only minor changes are needed from time to time, these can be made by means of a written statement (called a *codicil*) attached to the original document. The help of a lawyer is needed for amending a will.

How Can You Be Certain That the Distribution of the Estate Will Be without Problems?

You can make probate (the settling of the will) easier by following these simple procedures:

1. If you have made previous wills, tell your lawyer to destroy all earlier ones.

2. Choose a successor executor if your original choice cannot serve. Also, list contingent beneficiaries in the event your first choice may die before you or decline the inheritance.

3. In the event you have young children, pick a guardian in case they should become orphans.

4. Devise an order of payment if your estate becomes too small to pay all legacies.

5. Decide in advance whether the executor is to receive the standard compensation or a bequest from you.

6. Keep your will in a safe place (your lawyer's office and a copy at home) but preferably not in a safe deposit box; if the box is sealed upon your death, getting into it may be time-consuming and difficult. If you insist on the safe deposit box, open two of them and put your will in your spouse's safe deposit box and vice versa.

7. When making any bequest, leave a percentage of your estate rather than a fixed dollar amount because your assets may either grow or shrink over the years. However, you may wish to earmark specific sums for charities or certain heirs. Just remember that you will not be able to bequeath any property you own that is jointly held.

8. Make certain that your will is properly drafted or it may be interpreted in a manner that you did not wish. For example, if you want to disinherit a child (everywhere but Louisiana), be sure to specify in your will that you are doing it. If not, the child might later claim to have been overlooked by mistake. Don't use your will to throw your final insult at any individual; find some other means to "get even."

9. In certain situations, it's better to leave property in trusts rather than in outright bequests. A trust is simply an arrangement for transferring your title to your property (your ownership) to another person or company to hold in trust for you or anyone you designate. Trusts set up under a will are called *testamentary trusts* and become effective upon the death of the person who drew up the will. The trustee holds the property you otherwise would have bequeathed outright, and invests and administers it for the benefit of your stated beneficiaries. Trusts are frequently written into wills to ease the impact of estate taxes (particularly if a great deal of money is involved). There are countless ways of setting up trusts, so great care must be exercised to obtain the best possible legal tax advantages (see page 200 for alternatives to having a will).

Bear in mind that not all property goes through the courts (probate). In fact, a large portion of your estate is likely to pass outside probate court without any effort on your part. For example, the balance of your employee retirement plan, IRA, or Keogh account, as well as the proceeds of your life insurance policy, will go directly to your designated beneficiaries. Also, any property you own jointly with rights of survivorship will automatically go to the co-owner upon your death. If you live in one of the community property states (Arizona, California, Idaho, Louisiana, Nevada, Texas, and Washington), half of all your assets that you acquired during your marriage (except gifts or inheritances) belong to your spouse, with the other half passing under your will.

It is just as important for a wife to have a will as for her husband. A married couple often have interlocking or reciprocal wills prepared at the same time. These are separate documents carefully interrelated to one another and designed to meet the mutual objectives of both parties. For example, his-and-her wills should specify how the children are to be cared for in the event both parents die at the same time. And on the topic of marriage, how you own your money is just as important as knowing what you own. Transferring assets from one spouse to another might in some cases be your best financial move. For instance, a joint savings or checking account could be convenient today, but the surviving spouse might need those funds if the account is "frozen" when one of the account holders dies.

What Happens if You Die without a Will?

Without a will (*intestate*) you, in essence, have partially disinherited your spouse and condemned your estate to an unnecessarily prolonged and expensive wait. What happens is that your local court appoints an administrator to distribute your property in accordance with the laws of your state. A court-appointed professional administrator will receive between 3 and 5 percent of your estate in annual fees, thus giving the administrator little incentive to settle the estate quickly. If no blood relatives can be located, most states will claim ownership of the property. Also, if you are single, you need a will because without one all your assets would go first to your parents even though your brother, sister, or friends might need them more. Remember that making a will is one of the wisest investments of your life—and after.

Are There Any Alternatives to Having a Will?

One of the major drawbacks of a will is the cost and time to probate it. The process, at a minimum, can take 4 to 8 months, and if you have property in another state, or if any disgruntled relatives contest the will, your heirs might have to wait for years for the settlement. Also, administrative and legal costs during the probate process can run between 5 and 10 percent of the estate. The easiest way to avoid probate and have your assets transferred immediately is to set up a *revocable* or *living trust* (*inter vivos trust*), which transfers your assets to the trust while you are alive. When creating it, you must realize that you are required to switch the titles of everything you are placing in the trust from your name to the name of the trust. In every trust document, there are three principals. First, there is the *trustor*, who is the person or persons who created the trust and transferred the assets into it. Second, there is the *trustee*, who is the person or persons charged with the task of managing the assets in the trust. He or she makes all the financial and business decisions concerning the trust assets and has the right to buy, sell, trade, exchange, mortgage, and encumber. In fact, the trustee can do virtually anything with the trust assets except use them for his or her own benefit. These rights are reserved for the *beneficiary*, whose only responsibility is to use the assets.

When you create your trust, you can lawfully become all three parties: the trustor, the trustee, and the beneficiary. Under this arrangement, you can act as your own trustee, giving you control over your estate while you are alive. You then can appoint a successor trustee if you should become incapacitated or should die. Because the trust is revocable, it can be changed at any time you wish.

Unlike a will, a living trust can shield your estate from creditors. With a will, your executor is required to notify your creditors of your death by mail and newspaper advertisement so that they can submit any claims against the estate. No such publicity would take place in a living trust as no public notification is ever given. The trust avoids the courts and the general public. For example, when an estate goes through probate, the court freezes its assets for several months and gives notice that interested parties can come forward if they wish to contest the will. With a trust, no lawyer is needed. But to contest a trust, a disgruntled heir must hire a lawyer to file a civil suit. However, the assets of the trust are not frozen, and in many cases the trust is dissolved and assets distributed to the beneficiaries long before the disgruntled heir has a chance to act. He or she would then have to sue each beneficiary separately.

Although you do not have to go through the costly process of probate, the living trust is not without disadvantages.

1. By creating it, you would have to place everything you own into the trust. If you hold any assets outside the trust, you may have to go through probate anyway. You can remedy this drawback by placing any "outside assets" into joint ownership with right of survivorship.

2. It may cost more to establish a living trust than a will. Legal fees can be higher and assets must actually be transferred to the trust, which can create additional costs. Also, if you appoint another person as trustee, you will have to pay a fee in accordance with state law (unless the trustee waives the fee).

3. The right to choose your own fiscal year to defer taxes will be lost.

4. The trust funds must be used up before the creator can get any social service benefits (Medicaid, for example).

5. No tax advantage regarding estate taxes is gained by the revocable trust. Nor is there any income tax savings since all income from the trust passes through to the individual's personal income tax return.

6. You may need to have a simple will regardless of the living trust because you cannot use a trust to name a guardian for your minor children.

If you were to die tomorrow, the odds are that your heirs would be able to settle your estate without paying an inheritance tax because changes in federal and state tax codes have virtually eliminated the heavy "death taxes" for most of us. The federal exemption was only $60,000 in 1976 but now is $600,000. The federal tax is based on your taxable estate and the taxable portion of any gifts you made during your life. Adding taxable gifts to an estate is a way for the government to discourage people from dodging the federal estate tax by giving away all their property before they die. You can give up to $10,000 each year to as many people as you wish tax-free, and if your spouse joins in making the gift, $20,000 per recipient tax-free is permitted. The taxable portion of gifts is any amount over this annual exclusion.

For those of you who have large estates, there is a method of leaving these large funds without heavy federal taxation. By bequeathing the estate to your spouse, no tax is incurred. When the surviving spouse dies, tax is then applied to the beneficiaries of the estate over $600,000. However, by creating a bypass trust, you arrange to have up to $1,200,000 passed onto your children tax-free. Here's how it works. In your will you place up to $600,000 in a bypass trust and leave the rest to your spouse. In this way, the lifetime exemption ($600,000) and the unlimited marital deduction that is allowed shield the estate from federal estate taxes. The bypass trust pays income to your spouse and names the children as beneficiaries when the spouse dies. No control can be exercised by the spouse over the bypass trust. When the spouse dies, the amount of the trust is not part of the estate and so can be passed along (coupled with the spouse's estate up to $600,000) tax-free. And on the topic of estates, remember to get everything done before you are.

Epilogue

I hope that your reading of the material in this book has given you insight into the financial world and has taken the "utterly confused" status of investing into a more comprehensible realm. Bear in mind:

To look is one thing.

To see what you look at is another.

To understand what you see is a third.

To learn from what you understand is something else.

But to act on what you learn is all that really matters.

And that is the point. You must act now so that you can build a firm financial future for you and your family. Remember that the flowers of all tomorrows are in the seeds of today.

Glossary

adjustable-rate mortgage: A type of mortgage in which the interest rate charged may be changed at fixed intervals, usually in response to changes in some predetermined financial index.

annuity: A form of insurance in which the policyholder, called the *annuitant,* pays a specified sum of money and in return receives regular payments for the rest of his or her life.

appreciation: An increase in the value of any property; used especially in reference to an increase in the value of a stock, bond, or other security.

assay: To analyze gold or silver bullion and so determine the proportion of precious metal it contains.

back-end load: A sales fee or commission charged by the management of a mutual fund at the time the shares in the fund are sold. (*See also* front-end load.)

balloon mortgage: A type of mortgage in which the entire principal comes due within 2 to 5 years, at which time the loan must be repaid or refinanced at current interest rates.

banker's acceptance: A negotiable time draft (known as BA) used in international trade. It is also used as a safe short-term investment in the money market. It usually matures in 90 days and is guaranteed to be paid at maturity by the bank.

beneficiary: The person who receives financial benefit as a result of a will, an insurance policy, or a trust fund.

bond: An IOU issued by a corporation or government agency promising to pay a specified amount of interest for a specified period of time in exchange for an amount of money being lent to the corporation or agency.

broker: A person or firm engaged in buying or selling stocks, bonds, real estate, or other investment instruments on behalf of another person or firm. Brokers are normally licensed by one or more government agencies that monitor and regulate their activities.

bullion: Gold or silver of a specified purity, in the form of coins or, more commonly, bars or ingots.

bypass trust: A trust allowing the surviving spouse of the grantor to receive income from the property during the spouse's lifetime, after which the property passes to the grantor's other heirs.

callable bond: A bond which may be redeemed at the option of the issuing corporation or government agency before its maturity date.

capital: The total assets of a firm, including cash, land, buildings, equipment, investments, and accounts receivable.

capital gains: Profits from the sale of securities or real estate. Under the new Tax Reform Act, there is no longer any difference in the designation of long-term capital gain and short-term capital gain, as all gains are now treated the same. Prior to 1987, a long-term gain (held for more than 6 months) would receive favorable income tax treatment.

cash value: *See* surrender value.

certificate of deposit: A certificate representing an investment of a specified sum of money in a bank at a specified interest rate guaranteed for a particular period of time.

closing costs: Costs paid by the buyer of a home at the time of purchase. Closing costs include such charges as appraisal and surveying fees, title search costs, and lawyers' fees, and range from 2 to 10 percent of the purchase price of the home.

collateral: Property whose value is offered as a guarantee of repayment of a loan. If the loan is not repaid, the creditor is entitled to ownership of the collateral.

commercial bank: A bank which primarily serves business firms, although most commercial banks also accept deposits from and make loans to individuals.

common stock: A security that represents partial ownership in the issuing corporation. The holder of a share of common stock has the right to receive part of the company's earnings and to vote on certain policy decisions facing the company. (*See also* preferred stock.)

compound interest: Interest computed by applying the percentage rate not only to the principal but also to previously earned interest. The more frequently interest is compounded, the greater the effective yield of an investment.

condominium: A form of real estate ownership in which the owner holds the title to his or her own dwelling unit as well as a share in common properties such as lobbies, parking areas, and recreational facilities.

convertible bond: A corporate bond which may be exchanged at the option of the bondholder for shares of common stock in the same corporation.

cooperative: A form of real estate in which the owner buys one or more shares in a corporation that owns and manages land and buildings. Each share in the corporation entitles its owner to occupy part of the property, such as an apartment.

coupon bond: A bond with interest coupons attached that are clipped by the holder and redeemed at specified intervals for interest payments.

credit union: A savings institution that is owned by its depositors, who are technically considered shareholders. Like a savings bank, a credit union accepts deposits and makes loans, often at lower interest rates than those offered by banks.

creditor: A person or institution to which a debt is owed. The holder of a bond issued by a corporation, for example, is a creditor of the corporation.

custodial account: A savings or investment account, often in the name of a child, with another person, such as a parent, listed as custodian. The custodian manages the account, but the income belongs to the owner of the account and may normally be used only for his or her benefit.

debenture: A corporate bond whose value is not guaranteed by a pledge of collateral.

depreciation: A decline in the value of a piece of property over time. The depreciation of income-producing property is treated as a loss and so is deductible from income for income tax purposes; the amount of the tax deduction is computed by formulas that vary according to the nature of the property.

diversification: Investment of funds in a variety of instruments having differing yields, maturities, and degrees of risk. Diversification is generally considered a beneficial investment strategy.

dividend: A portion of a company's profits distributed to the stockholders. In a given year, a company's board of directors may or may not pay a dividend, depending on the company's financial status and anticipated future needs.

down payment: A partial payment for a piece of property, such as a home, made at the time of purchase, with the understanding that the balance will be paid later.

equity: The value of a piece of property to its owner over and above any portion of that value which has been offered as collateral for a loan. For example, the owner of a house worth $150,000 on which a $90,000 mortgage has been taken has $60,000 in equity.

executor: A person named in a will to manage the settlement of the estate according to the instructions given in the will.

401(k): Known as the deferred salary reduction plan, it allows an employee to set aside part of his or her salary (maximum $9500 or 25 percent of earnings) into a tax-sheltered account which grows tax-free until withdrawal.

face value: The value of a stock, bond, or insurance policy, usually printed on the front (or "face") of the document. The face value of a security usually differs from its selling price.

Federal Reserve: The central monetary authority of the United States. The Federal Reserve issues currency, sells U.S. government securities, and extends credit to member banks.

foreclosure: The process whereby the holder of a mortgage receives ownership of a property after the owner has failed to repay the loan.

front-end load: A sales fee or commission charged by the management of a mutual fund at the time the shares in the fund are purchased. (*See also* back-end load.)

income averaging: A method of computing income tax liability by which an unusually large amount of income received in a single year is spread out over several years, thus reducing the rate of taxation.

individual retirement account (IRA): A savings or investment plan which allows an individual to accumulate funds toward retirement while deferring income taxes on both the amount invested and the interest earned.

inflation: An increase in the general level of prices for goods and services in an economy.

insurance: A contract in which one party—usually a company organized for the purpose—promises to pay a specified sum of money in the event that the second party suffers a financial loss through death, accident, injury, or some other misfortune.

intestacy: The condition of dying without having made a valid will. When a person dies intestate, his or her estate is usually distributed in accordance with state laws.

junk bond: A corporate bond rated BB or lower by Standard & Poor's rating service or Ba or lower by Moody's rating service. Junk bonds carry a relatively high degree of risk but generally pay a high rate of return.

Keogh plan: A savings or investment plan for self-employed persons whose purpose and benefits resemble those of the IRA. However, the Keogh plan allows a larger amount of money to be sheltered from income taxes each year.

liquidity: The ease with which invested funds can be sold or otherwise converted to cash.

living trust: A trust which takes effect during the lifetime of the person who establishes it. At the death of the maker of the trust, probate is avoided and the assets are immediately transferred to the beneficiary.

load: The commission charged by the firm that manages a mutual fund; normally a percentage of the amount invested.

margin: Cash or credit advanced by a broker to allow the purchase of stocks or bonds for only a fraction of the full price. Making such a purchase is known as *buying on margin.*

maturity: The date on which a loan must be paid, or the period during which the loan may remain outstanding.

money market: The market in which various kinds of high-yielding, short-term securities are bought and sold. Interest rates on the money market respond quickly to changes in financial and economic conditions.

money market deposit account: A bank account whose funds are invested in money market securities.

money market fund: A mutual fund which invests in money market securities.

mortgage: A loan made with the ownership of personal property, such as a house, given as collateral. If the loan is not repaid, the holder of the mortgage has a right to ownership of the property.

municipal bond: A bond issued by a state or local government or one of its agencies. Interest earned on municipal bonds is normally exempt from federal income tax, and sometimes from state and local income taxes as well.

mutual fund: An investment company that pools the funds of many individuals and invests them in stocks, bonds, or other securities. Those who invest through a mutual fund are called *shareholders* and receive dividends whose size depends on the performance of the fund's investments.

no-load fund: A mutual fund that does not charge a commission on investments.

option: A contract giving the right to buy or sell a specified quantity of stock at a specified price within a specified period of time.

par value: The value printed on the face of a stock or bond; often the same as the initial selling price. The resale price of a stock or bond usually differs from the par value.

pension: An arrangement in which regular payments are made to a retired employee by his or her former employer or by a government agency.

points: An interest charge levied by a mortgage lender at the time a house is sold. For each point charged, the buyer must pay the lending institution 1 percent of the mortgage amount. On some mortgages, no points are charged; on others, 3 points or more.

portfolio: The complete array of investment holdings belonging to an individual or an institution.

preferred stock: A security representing partial ownership in the issuing corporation. Holders of preferred stock have a prior claim to the earnings and assets of the company over holders of common stock. Preferred stock usually carries no stockholder voting privileges and usually pays a pre-fixed annual dividend.

premium: (1) The amount of money paid to purchase a life insurance policy or an annuity. (2) The amount by which the selling price of stock or bond exceeds its face value or par value.

principal: An amount of money lent or invested.

prospectus: A formal document prepared by a corporation issuing stocks, bonds, or other securities that is made available to all prospective buyers of the securities. The prospectus must include certain facts about the company and the security as specified by the Securities and Exchange Commission, including the names of the corporation's officers, as well as the corporation's financial condition and its recent record of profits and losses.

redemption: The repurchase of a bond or other form of indebtedness by the issuing corporation or government agency.

registered bond: A bond registered in its owner's name. Interest is paid at regular intervals to the registered owner; the bond may be transferred only by changing the registration.

reinvestment: (1) The practice of returning all or some of a company's profits to the business for use in financing growth, plant, or equipment purchases. (2) An arrangement whereby dividends or interest earned by shares in a mutual fund is automatically used to purchase additional shares in the fund.

return on investment: The amount of profit received on an investment as a percentage of the amount of capital invested. Also called *yield*.

revocable living trust: A trust established during the grantor's lifetime in which a change or revocation can take place any time.

savings bank: A state-chartered financial institution which accepts deposits and offers loans at regulated interest rates.

savings and loan association: A financial institution, technically owned by depositors, which invests primarily in home mortgages.

Securities and Exchange Commission (SEC): The U.S. federal regulatory agency charged with controlling the issuing, buying, and selling of stocks, bonds, and other securities. The SEC supervises the operation of securities exchanges, registers brokers, and enforces laws governing the issuance of securities.

security: A written instrument that either certifies partial ownership of a business or promises repayment of a debt by a business or government agency.

shareholder: The owner of one or more shares of stock in a corporation or mutual fund.

simplified employee pension (SEP): A retirement plan for business owners, including those self-employed. An IRA is set up for each employee up to a maximum of $30,000 or 15 percent (13.043 percent if self-employed) of earnings.

single-premium whole life (SPWL): A single one-time premium that is paid at the beginning of the insurance policy (usually $5000 minimum). The policy offers excellent tax benefits.

stock: A share in the ownership of a corporation.

surrender value: The amount of money for which a life insurance policy may be redeemed prior to the death of the policyholder. In most cases, the surrender value of a policy increases annually during the life of the policy. Also called *cash value.*

tax bracket: The level at which an individual's income is taxed, normally determined by the size of his or her taxable income. The higher the taxable income, the higher the tax bracket and the higher the rate of taxation.

tax-deferred: Not subject to income tax until a later date.

tax-exempt: Not subject to income tax.

tax shelter: Any device or strategy by which a taxpayer can avoid paying income taxes on a portion of his or her income. Examples include individual retirement accounts (IRAs), Keogh plan accounts, 401(k) accounts, and certain limited partnerships.

term: The period of time during which an investment or an insurance policy is in effect.

term insurance: A form of life insurance in which the benefit is payable only if the insured person dies during a specified period.

testamentary trust: A trust which takes effect only after the death of the person who established it.

Treasury bill: A short-term obligation of the federal government, sold in minimum amounts of $10,000, with maturity periods of 3, 6, and 12 months. Treasury bills are sold at a discount from their face value; the discount represents prepayment of the interest on the loan. At maturity, the bill is redeemable for its full face value.

Treasury bond: A long-term obligation of the federal government, sold in minimum amounts of $1000, with maturity periods of 10 to 30 years. Treasury bonds are sold both by the federal government and in the secondary market, where the prices fluctuate in accordance with changes in interest rates.

Treasury note: An intermediate-term obligation of the federal government, sold in minimum amounts of $1000 or $5000 (depending upon maturity), with maturity periods of 1 to 10 years. Like Treasury bonds, Treasury notes are available on the secondary market at varying prices.

trust: An arrangement whereby property is transferred from one party, called the *grantor,* to a second party, called the *trustee,* for the benefit of a third party, called the *beneficiary.* Trusts are usually established in order to reduce tax liability, streamline the transfer of assets after death, and/or maintain some control over the use of assets after they have been transferred.

unit trust: An investment plan in which an investor buys a share in a portfolio of corporate or municipal bonds. The investor receives a specified rate of interest on his or her investment payable over a specified period of time, depending on the maturity dates of the bonds in the portfolio.

universal life insurance: A type of life insurance policy in which part of the premium payment is used to provide life insurance protection and the remainder is invested in any of a variety of high-yielding instruments.

volume: (1) The number of shares of a particular stock that are bought or sold on a given day. (2) The total number of shares of stock that are bought or sold on an organized exchange on a given day.

whole life insurance: A type of life insurance policy in which premium payments are continued at the same level throughout the life of the policyholder, with death benefits payable whenever the policyholder dies.

will: A written document prepared according to legal specifications which provides for distribution of the writer's assets after his or her death.

yield: *See* return on investment.

zero coupon bond: A corporate, municipal, or Treasury bond sold at a discount from its face value. Upon maturity, the zero coupon bond is redeemed for the full face value, with the discount representing the interest earned on the investment.